DEER CAMP
TALL TALES AND TIPS

Richard B. Tozier

Kennebec Fox

Published by Kennebec Fox
Skowhegan, Maine, USA

ISBN 1449904394   create-space.com

Printed in the United States of America

Kennebec Fox books by Richard B. Tozier:

Deer Camp Cooking Tall Tales and Tips

Cabin Fever: Poems and Ponderings

Figure 1: The Author

The author is 72 years young. He lives in Solon, Maine, in a home that is as close to a deer camp as he could make it. With his dog Mandy for company, he tends the wood stove. He writes poetry and has had one book of poems published, as well. This is his first attempt at writing a book.

Dedicated to:

The Boys of Kelly Brook

Figure 2: Kelly Brook Camp

Hunting is about food, not about keeping score.

Freedom is a Camp

There sets a camp on Kelly Brook,
Its history could fill a book.
The good time shared by all,
Winter-Spring-Summer-Fall.

Heaven should always be so near,
the fish-the birds-the white tail deer.
No electric-no bills-no telephone,
the law's long arm, left us alone.

What rules were made, we all agreed,
to save this place--to fill the need,
A need to have a life so free,
the way this life was meant to be.

Should you find "the life" you're leading,
lacking of the peace your needing,
find yourself a place like this:
a life of peace and days of bliss.

Introduction

I have tried to use no cuss words in the writing of this book. Cussing kind of goes with hunting, especially when things go wrong.

After you have pulled the trigger and the adrenalin has dropped back to normal, the work begins. This is a time when cussing seems to help matters.

A long cold night in the woods (when you could be back at camp-warm, dry and enjoying your favorite beverage) calls for a form of cussing that could be called "classic." At this time, words can be invented never before heard in the English language.

The American Dream

Most of my generation, after leaving the hallowed halls of learning, went off in search of the "American Dream." At the time this consisted of two cars in every garage and a yard bird in every pot.

My "American Dream" was a $200 Scout, its garage being anywhere I happened to park it, and deer meat in every skillet. I never much cared for yard bird anyhow.

Being able to look back over my misspent life with fond memories tells me I made the right choice for me. Money has never been an important part of my life and if I had some today, I would publish this book myself and give copies of it to anyone that wanted it. Money to me is nothing more than a tool and too much of it would become a burden that would require more time and effort than I would want to expend.[1]

Thought for the Day

If you worry about your dreams not coming true, just remember that your nightmares don't come true either.

---

[1] I have always believed that most of life's lessons are not learned from books.

The Kids and Me

From the time my son Dave was 10 years old, I took him out of school for a week every fall to go to deer camp with his Dad. He had to earn this trip by keeping his grades up before and after the trip. We still have our weeks hunting together to this day. The only years we missed were his years in the Marines.

My daughter Nancy was the fisherman in the family. She didn't care much for hunting. One of the few regrets that I have is that I never took her out of school for a weeks' worth of fishing. The only excuse I have is that at this time of year, I was at "work" on construction somewhere in North America.[2]

Figure 3: Me and my son Dave back in the Good old days (1966)

Fifty six years of living, working, and playing in the Maine woods, I think, gives me the background to write about the two subjects I know best: WHITETAIL DEER and COOKING.[3]

I started going with my dad on deer hunts at the age of five.

---

[2] Please excuse me for the four-letter words; I promised I would not use them in the book

[3] I used to be good at a third thing, but I had better not go into that in this epic. Tip #1: *If you feel that you have a need to write, write about what you know.*

My dad didn't care much for hunting. It was just another chore that had to be done so that we could eat through the winter months. I loved it; not so much the killing, but the woods lore and the hunting part.

There were times back in the fifties and sixties when what I learned help to feed my family. Times got better after that, as they most always do if you work at it.

I acquired Kelly Brook camp in the early sixties from my father-in-law Lynn Greenleaf of Skowhegan and it was the best present anyone ever gave me. Ron Greenleaf, my brother-in-law and the only brother I have ever had, was co-owner with me. If there is an Eden on earth, Kelly Brook camp was it (without Eve).

I started my son's training in the ways of the woods and the Maine whitetail deer at the age of five. What was good enough for me was good enough for him.

The time we spent at Kelly Brook created a bond between us that has lasted to this day. I don't hunt much anymore, but I relive the memories every day and now I would like to share them with you.

Getting to Camp

I started going to Kelly Brook camp back in the days before ATVs. The only way to reach the camp was a walk of about two miles. In all the years we used the camp, we never saw a game warden or another hunter, other than those of our party.

Backpacking to camp was hard work so a lot of life's luxuries were left behind. Drinks were served without ice. If icicles formed on the eaves or the brook froze over, we then could enjoy the good life.

Ron and me would pack supplies in about September and work up wood to get ready for deer season. There will be a story about one of these trips later on in the book.

It was nothing back then to carry large loads in on our backs and many's the time I've packed into camp with well over one hundred pounds on my back. Going in for the first hunt of the year, the boys would load up with more weight on their back than a jackass could carry without balking up. You would soon start seeing items left by the trail as the loads started to get lighter and sometimes it would be the next day before everything arrived at camp.

All of this work has its "pluses." The deer were large and numerous and fairly tame. Getting these large deer out to the trucks was another big job of work. I have shot the biggest deer of my hunting career in this area (some of these very close to camp, mind you.)

Being that no wardens ever came in to camp we were able to bend the game laws some, and in some cases "downright fracture them". In this book, we will discuss some of those tall tales.

The ideal deer camp should be located in a remote area. This allows for the bending of those dreaded game laws. It should be far removed from all watering holes, dance halls and anyplace where members of the female persuasion are to be found.

This will do away with any explaining you will need to do on returning home to the little women.

This is not to say that the boys didn't enjoy their favorite beverage, they did and in copious amounts.[4]

A remote location also separates you from the thundering herds of orange clad, heavily armed hunters who think the only way to get their deer is to "out number them".

The ideal deer camp should be free of carpets, curtains or any of the other things that require the "dreaded housework." The ideal deer camp should come equipped with a wood cook stove. However if your deer camp doesn't have one, some of the following recipes can be cooked on a heater stove.

Ironware works best for me when cooking on a wood stove. I also prefer enamelware cups and dishes. Breakage is not a problem. We had a bear get into the camp once and he broke every glass and dish in the place.

If your camp meets the above standards, cooking for a large group of hungry hunters full of their favorite beverages there will be no problem.

Deer Camp Tips

If you come across fresh deer sign, *don't grease the skillet just yet.* The recipes in this book are not all mine alone. Most of them have no name with them for who concocted them so I cannot give credit where credit is due. Wherever possible, the name will appear with the recipe.

The recipes I do claim as mine may have started with someone else, but I have changed them so much from the original that I think that I can claim them as my own.[5]

I always kept my deer camp well stocked with all the basics. There was always the chance of becoming snowed in. Everything has to be stored in mouse- and squirrel-proof containers. There are no bear-proof containers that I have found and you can believe we needed them more than once.

I found that kitchen trash bags, inside of potato chip cans worked very well. Canned goods can be kept from freezing by wrapping them in sleeping bags or bedding and hanging them from the rafters. This keeps the varmints out of your bedding.

Matches must be kept in dry and tight mouse-proof containers. Mice like to chew on them and this could cause a fire.

---

[4] I must add here this doesn't take place while hunting, only in the evening when the hunting has ended for the day.

[5] I love to improve on basic recipes.

Figure 4: The good old days: "camp meat"

Deer Camp Basic Staples List

Flour & sugar
Dry beans, dry mustard & molasses
Spices, salt & pepper
Dry milk & dry yeast
Bakewell™ Cream & baking soda
Instant potatoes
Canned goods
Powdered eggs
Coffee, tea & cocoa

Plus: your favorite beverage

Figure 5: Boys of Kelly Brook Camp: (left to right) Gerry Savage, Russ McLaughlin, "Sure-shot" Savage, Me, Dave McLaughlin, Jr.; Dave McLaughlin, Sr. took the picture (1966)

Comfort Kit

My thinking every trip into the woods I make (no matter what the reason for going) was that I might have to spend the night out doors, even though my plans were to return at the end of the day. There is also always the chance of injury or of becoming lost. The Maine woods can be a friendly place as long as you have respect for them. Mother Nature can and sometimes does, "jump up and bite you where you sit."

The following items go into my pockets, or sometimes a backpack, depending on my plans for the day. All of these items (with a little planning) will fit into your pockets-a fanny pack or a small backpack:

1. A compass and the know how to use it.
2. A map-if the country I am going to be is strange to me.
3. Waterproof matches in a watertight tin.
4. A candle: One about 4 inches long and 1 inch in diameter works best for me. Fire is the number one priority if you have to spend the night in the woods.
5. About 25 ft. nylon parachute cord: This is handy around an overnight camp and also for dressing and dragging your deer (if you are that lucky.)
6. A belt knife: This should have at least a 6-inch heavy blade for building a quick shelter and for firewood. I use a Buck Pro Line. This knife holds an edge very well.
7. A lock-back pocket or belt knife for dressing and skinning game: For years I carried a Barlow knife sold by Sears & Roebuck back when their

catalogues were still used in out-houses. Case has come out with what I think is the best all-around knife on the market today, however: it has 3 interchangeable blades and a small saw blade. I carried one of these the last few years, however I still kept my Buck knife with me for heavy work.

8. 3 or 4 small boxes of raisins: These are high-energy food that will help to keep you warm during a long cold night.

9. A small flashlight that takes AA batteries--make sure these are fresh.

I also took with me an Alka-Seltzer bottle full of brandy. This does nothing for you except give you a feeling of well being on a long cold night in the woods.

This may seem like a lot of tonnage to carry around with you, but these few items can make all the difference between a miserable or a pleasant night in the woods. I have spent a few unplanned nights in the woods so I know of what I speak.

Enjoy your hunt knowing that you are prepared for most anything that comes your way.

A Tip to Remember

I was hunting with my dad one day when I was about knee high to a short frog. It was a cold November day with a rain and snow mix and by noon our woolens were soaked and heavy. At noontime my Dad crawled under a fir blow-down and with his belt knife, cut some tinder from the underside where the rain didn't hit. He then found a spruce tree with limbs almost too the ground. When we got under that, we had shelter.

Removing a match from his waterproof case, he said "I am going to show you how to light a fire in the rain with just one match." He then took a candle from his pocket. He lit the candle with the match and lit the tinder. With dead limbs from the bottom of the spruce, we had a small smokeless fire. We were soon warm and getting dry.

The Old-Timers

My Dad was a good teacher when it came to woods lore and the care and safety of firearms. My Granddad was a hunter for the logging camps back when this was legal. What he gave to me was the ability to find fish and game: to know their habits and put meat on the table every time I needed to do so.

I had uncles that did nothing but fish, hunt and trap. I could and did sit for hours and listen to them tell their stories. They never worked for another man or worked inside all their lives.

Those old-timers were responsible for most of what I know of the woods and surviving in them today.

Any chance that you get to hunt with or listen to the old-timers, take these opportunities and really pay attention, your life will be better for it. I guess I would be considered one of the "old-timers" now.

You are probably wondering about now, "where are the game recipes?" The days of getting a deer for camp meat are long gone, unless you are very lucky. And should you get so lucky, just use deer meat in the recipes put forth in this book.

There are many game cookbooks on the market today--I own a few of them myself. There is no need to repeat their titles here. I do however have some tips on cooking deer meat that I have not seen in any cookbooks so far.

By the way: up here in Maine, we do not call deer meat "venison."

Deer meat has no food value. If you had only deer meat to eat, you would starve to death on a full stomach. If you were to use every part of the deer as the Native Americans did, then you could survive (this includes the blood, the tongue, the bone marrow and the internal organs.) In this cookbook, I will give you some tips on using parts of the deer that you probably throw away.

Basic Recipes

Camp Jerky

If we were lucky enough to have a small deer for camp meat, I would make what I called "camp jerky." This is not a true jerky, mind you, because true jerky requires smoke. This jerky however is easy to make and disappears like peanuts-- "you can't eat just one."

- I would remove a cut of meat from the front quarter of the camp meat deer, (these will be small in diameter.)
- Slice thin and roll in salt, pepper, and garlic powder.
- Brown these in a skillet with no grease. Remove and place on a cookie sheet or in a metal pie plate if you have a wood cook stove.
- Set these on the back of the stove to dry.

If you do not have a wood cook stove, hang them on a string over heat to dry.

Deer & Beer

This is a good way to cook stew meat, but first, let's partake of our favorite beverage, which in this case, is a good choice.

1.   Roll meat in salt and pepper and brown in a large iron skillet than add:
3-potatoes (halved)
3-carrots (sliced)
1-onion (diced)

2.   Into a large bowl put:
1-cup beer
¼ cup chili sauce
2 tbsp brown sugar
1 clove garlic (minced)
½ cup cold water
3 tsp flour
½ tsp salt

3.   Pour into skillet, adding more beer, if needed.
4.   Simmer one hour.
5.   Remove mixture and place in a Dutch oven.
6.   Add more beer, if needed, and bake until potatoes are done.

Deer Heart

I am told that the liver of the deer is now toxic and unfit to eat so I will now get right to the heart of the matter.

Maybe the heart is toxic also, I don't know. I do know it is one of the best eating parts of the deer and I am going to eat it anyway. There are quite a few hunters that leave this fine eating in the woods. If you are one of these hunters, please bring all deer hearts to me from now on.

1. Soak the heart overnight in cold water.
2. Cut into ¼ inch thick slices.
3. Sauté in butter, cooking sherry and a dash of lemon juice.
4. Serve with eggs and home fries for breakfast.

Deer Tongue

The tongue is a part of the deer that most hunters throw away. This is a pity because tongue is one of the most flavorful parts of the animal.

1. Boil the tongue and skin it as you would a beef tongue.
2. Slice it about ¼ inch thick.

3. Sauté in butter-garlic and a splash of cooking sherry.

This goes very well with eggs or baked beans and also makes a great sandwich.

Deer Bones

These are a part of the deer that almost everyone throws away. If you are one of these hunters you are missing a real treat.

1. Boil the bones until you can remove the marrow. This is one of the few parts of a deer that has a food value.
2. Freeze the marrow and then thaw it so you can add it to soups and stews

The bone marrow will give these dishes a flavor you have probably never experienced.

Deer Roasts

I don't put much of my deer into roasts, but if you do, here are some tips that will help to keep them from being so dry.

Tip 1. Cook your deer roast beside a pork roast. The moisture from the pork will moisten the deer roast.
Tip 2. Place bacon strips under and on top of the roast and baste the roast with the bacon fat while cooking.
Tip 3. Cook roasts in a crock pot or in the oven in a large roaster, adding:
1 cup water
1 cup orange juice
1 large onion

Cook slowly until done.

Deer Burgers

Most of the deer that I get goes into steaks and stew meat. All of the meat left over I put into deer burger or sausage. If I was lucky enough to get two deer, I made sausage with one and deer burger with the other.

Deer burger by itself is very dry. I mix in the following ratio of 10 lbs. ground deer meat to 3 lbs. ground chuck and 2 lbs. fresh pork.

You can take the above amounts, add sausage seasonings, make patties and freeze them. They make very good sausage.

Moose Meat Marinade

Into a glass or casserole dish, mix-½ cup oil and vinegar or Italian dressing, which ever you prefer, adding:

> ¼ cup soy sauce
> 1 tsp hot sauce
> ¼ cup vermouth
> 1 large garlic clove (minced)
> 1 tbsp Worstershire sauce

Add meat and put in the fridge for 6-8 hrs.
Turn meat often.
Place in the oven at 350 degrees.
Baste with the marinade until done.

If you add a little flour to the pan drippings, you will have a very good gravy.

As you already have the vermouth, this is a good time for a martini, "shaken not stirred."

Bear Meat

It's been a long time since I have been hungry enough to shoot a bear. If you should get one, remember, a bear is nothing more than a hairy pig so treat the meat the same way you do pork.

If you should get a bear in a year with a bumper crop of beechnuts, render down the fat as your would lard. It makes the best piecrust you have ever eaten.

Today a bear is worth quite a lot of money. The teeth and claws are used to make jewelry. Some cultures that use the internal organs as a stimulant for increasing sexual prowess pay well for these organs.[6]

---

[6] This never worked for me. As a bear only gets his loving once a year I guess they didn't do him much good either.

Partridge

These birds are very dry so the cooking of them requires some moistening. I like to fry them in butter until they are golden brown. Frying them in bacon fat is also very good.

If I should have a bird when I am baking beans, I debone the bird and add it to the beans while they are baking.

When roasting a bird, I have found that if you stuff the bird with fruit cocktail, this will not only moisten the bird but also give an entirely different flavor.[7]

Game Pie

For this dish, you will need two or three different types of game, (the more the better.) I like to use rabbit, partridge and deer burger, but any game or any meat works well. Squirrels are very good if you can bring yourself to shoot one of these cute little fellas--I can't.

You need a large pie plate and a double pie crust, rendered down bear fat from a bear that has been feeding off of beechnuts will give you the light and fluffy pie crust that you have been striving for, if you are like me, for your whole life.

Debone the meat and sauté in butter, garlic, onions, wine and a dash of lemon juice.

I myself do not use vegetables, but any veggie you wish works great. Once in awhile I will use spinach for a change of pace. When I use this, I put a layer of cheese on the top just below the crust.

Add poultry seasoning and sage to your taste. Other spices can be used, as this is a good dish to play around with.

Moose, ala Kelly Brook

The best way to make this dish is to have someone donate the moose meat. By the time you have worked up your own moose you will eat it any way its cooked.

Wine is the beverage of the day.

You will need:

> Some part of a moose (about 2 lbs.)
> 1 can mushroom soup
> ½ cup more or less burgundy wine
> 3-4 pinches ground parsley

---

[7] A cocktail for you while the bird is cooking makes this dish much better.

a pinch of pepper
1 can cocktail onions
2 cups sliced mushrooms

Cube your moose and brown in olive oil. Drain off oil and add first 5 ingredients. Simmer for 1½ hrs. Add the rest of the ingredients and more wine if needed. Simmer 1more hr.

This goes very well with rice or pasta.

One Pot Deer Roast

This is another of those recipes that will take the dryness out of a deer roast. The more beverages consumed the better it will taste. You will need:

1 3 or 4 lb roast.
1 cup flour.
½ tsp pepper.
1 tsp salt.
3 medium onions (sliced)
1 clove garlic (scrunched)
4-6 carrots.
5-6 medium potatoes
hot sauce to taste.
1 Dutch oven.

Mix: flour, salt and pepper and rub into roast. Place in hot Dutch oven and brown on both sides. Cover with water, and then add veggies and hot sauce. Cook until the meat separates easily and veggies are done.

This dish is great for the campfire or on the grill but it can be cooked on any stove either on a burner or in the oven.

Deer Meat in Sauce

A large part of the deer can be used as stew meat, so the more stew recipes you have, the better.
This dish I concocted on one of my slow days, of which I have quite a few. As you will be using wine for this dish why not make it the beverage of choice.
First you will need to get you a deer, one way or another.
You will need these ingredients:

2-3 lbs. stew meat.
2 green peppers (diced)
1 cup water
1 cup wine
1 tsp salt
1 can chunk pineapple.

Sauce:
4 tbsp corn starch
½ cup sugar
4 tbsp soy sauce
1½ cups pineapple juice

Brown the meat on all sides. Add water and salt and cook until meat is done, adding water as needed as it cooks.

Boil the peppers and add to the skillet. Add the pineapple and a little wine.

Make the sauce by mixing all sauce ingredients and simmer until the sauce thickens. Add this to the skillet and simmer all for 5-10 minutes. You can serve this dish over rice, noodles, or potatoes.[8]

---

[8] Try not to leave any wine in the bottle as this tends to ruin the meal and besides the bottle is worth 15¢.

My Own Wood Duck Recipe

This is my famous recipe for roasting a wild duck.

First go out and shoot yourself a duck.

As soon as you have done this, enjoy a favorite beverage. If this took all day you maybe will want more than one? When you have fortified yourself with the beverages to proceed, dress and skin the duck. We won't be cooking with beverages at this time as you will need all that you have too get through this ordeal.

The next thing that you need to do is find a rock that weighs exactly the same as the duck. Place the duck and the rock in a roasting pan and put them both in the oven at the highest temperature your oven will go.

If you are still enjoying a beverage, check the duck and the rock often.

When you can stick a fork in the rock the duck is ready to be served (as likely, is the rock.)

If you have consumed enough beverages at this time, you will maybe enjoy this dish.

Figure 6: Denny Robbins and me and some of those wild ducks

Figure 7: The Camp Dishwasher in Full Uniform

The Kelly Brook Outhouse

I was told that the Kelly Brook outhouse came into being in 1937, coincidentally, the same year that I came into being.

It started out as a modest and unimposing structure, about the size of a telephone booth without the windows. The throne was two feet off the ground.

When we inherited the camp, this noble edifice was leaning about six inches off the plumb. The roof leaked so badly that if it rained you had automatic flush. The boards were shrunk so much you could accomplish your mission and watch for deer at the same time.[9]

The door had long since fallen off, so privacy was sadly lacking. The wind blowing thru the cracks was music to the ears. The seat that started at two feet from the ground was now located at about a foot. Yes, I mean the ground--the floor had long since rotted away.

Every year we held a board meeting to discuss what to do about fixing it up or building a new one. As all building materials had to be backpacked in, the consensus was that it was good for another year.

About 3 AM, one cold and frosty morning, Mother Nature gave me a serious wake up call. Knowing that Mother Nature could not be ignored for very long I made the trip to what we affectionately called "the head office."

Reaching my destination I dropped my laundry and gently lowered myself on to what I thought would be a very cold seat. What I sat on was a very upset hedgehog.

With my pants down around my knees, I returned to the safety of the camp. With some help from my friends, we removed the quills from the area that I couldn't

---

[9] Your rifle was standard equipment on these trips.

reach, all the time discussing this turn of events in a language entirely new to the English-speaking people.

As soon as first aid was completed I grabbed the chainsaw and cut this noble structure to the ground.

As far as I was concerned a blow-down out back in the woods was more privacy and protection than, "THAT DAMNED OUTHOUSE," and anyone who wished was more than welcome to build a new one.

There is no outhouse there to this day.

Figure 8: The Camp gets a new window (one of those Sunday jobs to take a break from hunting.)

The Family at Camp

The first weekend after Bub and me became the proud owners of the Kelly Brook camp, I decided to take my wife, Corrine, and spend my first weekend there with her. I couldn't wait to show off our new possession. This idea didn't do anything to bring much excitement into her life. Being a good wife who took the oath that said "for better or worse" seriously, she agreed (with some fast talking from me) to make the trip.

To entice her into this adventure, the two-mile hike became just a short walk in the woods. The brook became a beautiful stream; the camp became a backwoods "Howard Johnsons."

Right about here you can see the start of a successful career as a politician for me somewhere down the road.

After a lot of "how much furthers" and "my feet are killing me," we arrived at what had now become the second love of my life. She took a quick look around at these new surroundings and said, "pour me a drink and make that a double."

She informed me at this time that she would "never darken the door of that obscene structure called an outhouse." She would consent to go out back of the camp instead of using the floor, although she informed me the floor was her first choice. What that she didn't tell me was that come dark she would not set foot out of the camp even if it was on fire.

You can see from all of this that this girl is not that much at home in these types of situations.

My little second honeymoon at deer camp is about to turn ugly. I have now become bartender, cook, dishwasher and all around house mouse. If I am very lucky, maybe I can sleep in the bed, just not necessarily the same bed she is in, however.

There was at the camp, what I considered to be one of the essentials of any deer camp and essential too life itself. This was a very old gray enamel coffee pot. You fill this with cold water and bring it to a boil, add a handful of coffee (more or less), a pinch of salt and boil until done. Add cold water to settle the grounds and you have what I think is a good cup of coffee.

This coffee was high-octane and the leftovers could be used to run the chain saw.

Upon arising the next morning with the good intentions of making a pot of this outstanding coffee and thereby getting back in the good graces of my long suffering wife, I realize that I can't seem to find the coffee pot. I was forced to use one of the new-fangled pots that people seem to be so fond of.

When my wife finally decided to talk to me again, I asked her if she had seen the coffee pot. She claimed that she "…hadn't but she had found an old gray pot that didn't look to be good for much of anything and used it for nature calls and that I could find it under the bed. Would you be so good as too dump it while you're at it?"

As soon as my kids were old enough, they went to camp with me every chance they got.

My son Dave, being a chip off the old block, took to this like a duck to water. My daughter Nancy enjoyed the fishing and the wild life.

The woods were full of Whiskey Jacks. These birds are friendly to the point of being pests. Nancy would set on the chopping block in the yard and feed these camp robbers for hours. She would have birds in her hands, on her head and in her lap.

The pictures of these times were lost in a fire at one of our other camps, but we still have the memories.

No More Camp Meat

Figure 9: Gerry Savage with a spike-horn buck; the bear was camp meat.

It used to be that you could legally take a deer for camp meat. That is now against the law, as most good things are. We however continued this old tradition right up to the time that game started to become scarce. This was due to: coyotes, clear cutting and wolves. The spraying of toxic chemicals didn't do much to help matters any either.

Because of all of the above, I created the following recipe.

"We Got Skunked" Slumgullion

The first thing to do on the first day at deer camp is to enjoy your favorite beverage. While enjoying your second beverage, into a large soup kettle put one of quart water. Add to this:

> 3 large onions diced.
> 1 tbsp salt
> 1 tsp pepper
> 4-6 beef bullion cubes
> 6 cloves garlic, crushed
> 2 tbsp barley

Spices are your choice. This is a good recipe to experiment with. I like to add 4 tbsp Worstershire sauce and 2 tbsp hot sauce.

Leftover meat and vegetables from your meals are added to the kettle all week.

Any small game you hunters may bring in can be prepared and added to the kettle also.

The beauty of this dish is: it gets better by the day and the flavor changes from day to day. Anyone who wants a lunch at any time just dips into the kettle.

You will need to add liquid as the week goes by. Water, beer or wine will all work well.

Camp Breads

Because of the backpacking involved to reach our deer camp, store-bought bread didn't stand the trip very well. So I made biscuits and yeast rolls in double batches.

One year, I tried packing frozen bread dough into camp. By the time I arrived at camp the dough had thawed and I had me one large lump of dough, ready to bake "right now."

Bannock

This recipe comes from the colder parts of the country so if you feel a chill while making this dish, a hot buttered rum will do a good job of warming things up. You will need:

> 2½ cups of flour
> ¼ cup milk or powdered milk
> 1 cup water
> 2 eggs or 2 tbsp powdered eggs
> ½ tsp salt
> 2 tsp Bakewell™ Cream
> 1 tbsp melted grease or oil (I use peanut oil)

Mix well all the dry ingredients. Add liquids and oil and mix until the flour is wet. Knead 4-5 times. Place dough into a greased iron skillet and cook until golden brown.

Berries can be added to this for a camper's dessert.

Sky-High & Feather-Light Yeast Rolls

The first thing to do as with any good recipe is to enjoy your favorite beverage. Wine is a good choice as the bottle makes for a very good rolling pin.

I had to use powdered milk in place of what comes directly from the cow (the backpacking problem arises again.)

Different flours require more or less liquid, depending on the brand used. I get the best results with Pillsbury's™ bread flour.

You can add more milk or more flour during the mixing process.

You will probably have to make these at least every other day as they tend to disappear very fast.

Now that you have enjoyed your favorite beverage you may begin.

Into a saucepan, put 1¼ cups milk. then add 4 tbsp peanut oil, 2 tbsp sugar and ¼ tsp salt.

Stir and heat to lukewarm.

Into ½ cup warm water, add 2 packages dry yeast and dissolve. Add to warm milk mixture and stir.

Into a large mixing bowl, put 4 cups flour. Stir milk mixture into the flour, cover with a cloth and let rise 50 min.

You now have time to enjoy a beverage.

Place dough onto a floured surface and knead 6 to 8 times. Roll out dough to about ½ inch think and cut. I use a tuna fish can.

Dip in melted butter and fold in half.

Put rolls into a greased baking pan and let rise 20 minutes, uncovered.

You now have time for a few more beverages. Right about now things should be looking really rosy, (ain't cooking loads of fun?)

Bake the batch at 475 degrees for 20 minutes, or until done. If you're using a wood cook stove, I suggest that you keep a close eye on them at this stage of the operation, especially if you are still enjoying your favorite beverage.

Your rolls are now done. All that is left for you to do is avoid the stampede of hungry hunters.

The Ultimate Biscuit

I used to make baking powder biscuits until I discovered Bakewell™ Cream. This is a Maine product so if you are leaving Maine take a good supply with you.

The recipe on the can make great biscuits; however, I have changed this recipe over the years to make them even better.

With your favorite beverage in hand follow the directions on the can.

Use bread flour. For shortening, use peanut oil. Use more milk than called for. Your dough should be moist and sticky. Knead 6 to 8 times. After you have rolled them to about ¾ inch thick cut them with the ever-ready tuna can, brush with butter and let rise 20 minutes to ½ hr before baking.

Try butter and horseradish on these for a real treat.

Baked Beans, Done Easy

Most everyone has a recipe for baked beans, however mine is a little different so I am going to add it to the book. Some think that "more is better" so they add many things to their beans. My hunters like theirs simple. Once I made my beans with the correct ingredients, I had no leftovers.

First, have yourself a beverage of your choosing.

Soak 2 cups of dry beans (any type) overnight. Put into your bean pot-½lb. salt pork (or you can substitute 2-4 tbsp of olive oil, which may be healthier,) 2 tbsp molasses per cup of beans and 2 tbsp dry mustard.

Now comes the secret: add 1 tbsp ground coffee. Fill the pot with the water from the soak.

I don't know if instant coffee will work as well. I do know that if I had to drink instant coffee, I would become a tea drinker.

If you are lucky enough to have a partridge at this time, bone it out and add it to the pot. You will make friends for life.

The yeast rolls really compliment this dish and the coffee added too the pot makes for a perfect juice for sopping the rolls in.

Kelly Brook Country Fried Steak

Besides your beverage you will need:

> 1 cup buttermilk – dry
> 4 4-oz. cube steaks
> 1 ¾ cups flour, divided
> ½ tsp garlic powder
> salt and pepper to taste
> 2 tbsp oil (I use olive oil)
> 2 cups milk or powdered milk

Pour buttermilk into a medium-sized bowl. Add meat and gently coat each piece. Combine 1 ½ cups flour, garlic powder, salt and pepper in a plastic bag. Take meat out of buttermilk and shake to remove excess liquid. Place the meat in the bag, close top and shake to coat with flour. Heat oil in skillet. Place a steak in skillet over medium-high heat. Brown on one side, turn and brown other side. Remove from skillet and keep warm while making gravy.

Cream Gravy:

1. Combine ¼ cup flour and 2 cups of milk in a jar with a lid and shake until flour is blended in. Pour into skillet in which the meat was cooked.
2. Stir to loosen bits of flour stuck to the pan Cook over low heat until gravy is thickened.
3. Season to taste with salt, pepper and hot sauce.

This is a good way to cook the poorer steaks from your deer (pound the living day-lights out of them first.) This technique also works well for cooking deer burger.

Biscuits are a must for sopping up the gravy.

Mountain Man Chili

This dish will put hair on your chest, improve your love life, and when you reach the end of the trail, no embalming will be required.

Your beverage should be cold, very cold. I prefer cold beer to cool the palette while sampling the dish for taste as it progresses. This dish can be blamed for some strange aromas wafting around the deer camp.

Into a large skillet, sauté in olive oil 4 large onions and 6 to 8 cloves of garlic sliced thin (I use a single edge razor blade to get them real thin.)

When these are transparent, remove from skillet and brown 3 to 4 lbs. of hamburg in olive oil. Into a large pot, put the above and then add:

4 21 oz cans Mexican style stewed tomatoes
8 jalapeno peppers (diced)
8 chili peppers (diced)
4 7 oz cans tomato paste
4 8 oz cans tomato sauce
2 green peppers (diced)
2 red peppers (diced)
1 tbsp cumin
1 tbsp cayenne pepper
4 tbsp hot sauce
1 tsp salt
¼ cup Worcestershire sauce
1 cup brown sugar
½ cup vinegar
½ cup tequila is optional

Let pot simmer all day on the back of the stove. The longer this cooks the better it gets!

This is a great recipe to experiment with. I have two more recipes that I have come up with from this basic recipe. Put some of this into a casserole dish, cover the top with cheese, and bake. This is not only a very good main dish; it also makes a good party dip and very good chili dogs.[10]

Molasses Cookies

My hunters at deer camp had a sweet tooth as much as anyone so I made pies and cakes, mostly from cans and boxes. There was one recipe that was given to me by Methyl Bonneau of Skowhegan. The boys couldn't get enough of these. I made them by the double batch and couldn't keep them in the camp. They are simple to make and even if you should be missing some ingredients they still come out good. Into a large mixing bowl, put:

> 6 cups flour
> 1 cup molasses
> 1 cup oil
> 1 egg
> 1 cup sugar
> 1 tsp ginger
> 1 tsp cinnamon
> ¼ tsp ground cloves
> 1 cup brewed coffee or
> 1 cup sour milk

To the coffee, add:

> 4 tsp baking soda
> 1 tbsp vanilla

Mix all together. Mixture must be stiff. Roll ½ inch thick and cut with the ever-popular tuna fish can. Place on an ungreased cookie sheet and bake for 10 minutes or until done.

Potato Dumplings

I forget who gave me this recipe. Wherever it came from, I like it as it is quick and easy, and there are usually potatoes left over. You need the equal of about 4 potatoes, (mashed).

> 2 cups bread or cracker crumbs
> ¼ cup of milk
> 1 small grated onion

---

[10] Also, try this chili on pizza crust.

Mix these together. Beat two eggs and add to this:

> 1 tsp flour
> ½ tsp salt
> ¼ tsp pepper

Mix and add to the potato mixture. Blend well and shape into balls, any size you want. Roll balls in flour and drop into salted, boiling water and cover. These are done in about 15 minutes.

Skillet Bread

This is a very simple bread to make so it is ideal for camping trips as well as at deer camp. Freeze the dough and you are ready for any trip at any time.

When ice fishing or cold weather camping I fry this in bacon fat as fat helps keep you warm in cold temperatures.

Mix together:

> 6 cups flour
> 1 cup raisins
> 3 tbsp Bakewell™ Cream
> ¾ cup lard or peanut oil
> ½ tsp salt
> 2-3 cups water

Flatten dough to about 1 inch thick. Cook in greased iron skillet until brown.

Johnny Cake

It is said that "pea soup and Johnny cake will always make your belly ache" so you won't find a recipe for pea soup here.

Mix until very smooth:

> 2 large eggs
> 1 cup milk
> ¼ cup peanut oil
> 3/4 cup corn meal
> 1 cup flour
> 1 tsp salt
> 3 tsp Bakewell™ Cream
> 2 tbsp sugar

Pour into greased iron skillet and bake at 400 degrees for 20 minutes.

Warm this up for breakfast with butter and maple syrup.

Potato Biscuits

If you are running short of flour this is a very good biscuit to make. Instant mashed potatoes work well and these can be kept at camp with no storage problems if you followed the tips under the section on stocking your camp.

Mix together:

1 cup peanut oil
1 cup mashed potato
1 quart scalded milk
½ cup sugar
1 pack dry yeast
2 tsp salt
1 tsp baking powder
1 tsp baking soda

You can use Bakewell™ Cream in place of the last 2 ingredients. Mix first 3 ingredients and let cool. Add yeast dissolved in warm water and sugar. Add enough flour to make a batter. Let rise and then add salt, soda and baking powder.

Beat batter thoroughly and add flour to make biscuit dough. Let rise and cut into biscuits. Let rise again. Bake 10 minutes at 475 degrees or until done.

Sheppard's Pie

I have seen a lot of recipes for this dish, but none like the one to follow.

This recipe was passed down from my grandmother to my mother so I know it is very old.

As this recipe makes deer burger fit to eat and as this is a book on hunting, I will add it here.

Any type of ground meat works well in this dish.

In a large skillet, sauté 2 medium onions in butter until transparent.

Brown about 2 lbs ground meat in butter.

In a large baking pan or casserole dish, put a layer of the meat and onions. Next put a layer of your favorite veggie, (I like green beans or spinach).

Mix together 2 cans tomato soup and 1 can water and pour over meat and veggies.

Next add a layer of mashed potatoes, (about 3 or 4 cups). I like to sprinkle the top with bread or cracker crumbs (optional.)

Bake at 250 degrees until the potatoes start to brown.

Spices? Be creative.

Sweet or Hot B-B-Q Sauce

This recipe was given to me by my mother-law, Jeanne Greenleaf. I have added to this recipe until it is quite different from the original.

I make this sweet for pork and hot for beef and chicken.

I like a lot of garlic; maybe you will wish to cut back on this.

I also sample this dish from time to time as it simmers and add what I think is needed. If you choose to do this, your favorite beverage should be a cold one to cool off the palate.

It will be hard to give accurate amounts of the ingredients as I just add the basics and then fine-tune it as I go along.

By this time the reader should be familiar with the first step the cook needs to take before starting any recipe so let's proceed.

Into a large pot, put 1-28oz. bottle of ketchup, then pour ½ cup of vinegar into the empty ketchup bottle and shake. (I do this so as not to waster the ketchup that stays in the bottle). Add this to the pot.

Sauté garlic: (I use 12-15 cloves) in olive oil until transparent. Add to pot. Now add:

> ½ cup sugar (add another ½ cup brown sugar for pork.)
> ¼ cup Worcestershire sauce
> 2 tbsp hot sauce
> 1 tsp cumin
> 2 tsp cayenne pepper

Simmer for not less than 2 hrs.; longer is better. Stir often. The fine-tuning is done at this time and thru the simmering stage.

If you have sinus problems, a head cold or most anything else wrong with your head, inhale while cooking for instant relief. It has been said by some to have even helped their love life.

A Very Adaptable Stuffing

This stuffing works very well with all types of meat and fish.

I never can seem to make a small batch, but it still disappears as fast as I can make it.

Sauté in butter until transparent:

> 2 medium onions diced
> 4 celery stalks (sliced thin)
> 2 cups mushrooms (diced)

You can add a little wine to the skillet if you wish.
Into a large bowl put:

> ½ loaf dry or lightly toasted white bread, crumbled, or scrunched if you prefer
> ½ package soda crackers (scrunched)
> 1 package Ritz™ crackers (scrunched)
> 2 cups warm milk
> 2 eggs
> ½ stick melted butter
> 4 tbsp sage
> 4 tbsp poultry seasoning

You may have to add more of these (add to taste.)

Mix well and set in the fridge until ready to bake. This will add to the flavor.

When baking fish I add shellfish to the stuffing. Any type works well.

Taking a strip from the back loin of a deer about a foot long, I slice it in half along the length of it, put a layer of stuffing in the middle and a layer on top and bake. This makes a moist and tasty roast.

Hearty-Meaty Stew

In a large skillet, brown 2lbs. meat in flour and butter.

Into a large soup kettle put:

> 4 cups water
> 4 beef bouillon or chicken cubes
> 2 medium onions
> 6-8 carrots (sliced)
> 3-4 large potatoes (cubed)
> 4-6 tbsp Worcestershire sauce
> 1 tbsp hot sauce
> 1 tsp cumin
> a pinch of basil
> a pinch rosemary
> a pinch thyme
> 2 tbsp barley

Bring to a boil and then simmer all day.

I have used diced pumpkin in this and found it excellent.

I have also used 2 cans stewed tomatoes for a change of pace. This is another of those dishes, fun to play around with.

Kelly Brook Stir Fry

This simple recipe works well with all kinds of meat and fish. It works especially well with left-overs. Into skillet put ¼ lb. butter. When melted, add:

> 1 clove garlic, (sliced thin)
> 4 tbsp soy sauce
> ½ tsp hot sauce
> ¼ cup dry vermouth

Veggies and meat should be sliced thin and added to the skillet, stirring often. If using fish add a dash of lemon juice.

Serve over rice or mashed potatoes.[11]

Tall Tales

The Whitetail Deer

When the mother of us all made the white tail deer, she strived for perfection. She gave the deer a pair of ears probably equal to the best sonar system known to man. A nose that can pick up scents for great distances, speed for short distances and the agility to jump blow downs, fences and I once saw a deer jump over an automobile. She made the deer one of the most beautiful and graceful animals to be found anywhere on earth. And then, she threw two jokers into the deck: she gave these fine animals eyes that can only see quick movement and at very close range, and a curiosity that gets them killed.

I for one have found no honor in killing one of these magnificent creatures.

There has never been a deer that I have killed that I didn't cry after the deed was done. This I am not ashamed of.

I have seen hunters (mostly those not from around here) who tie a deer they have shot to their car or truck and parade around from bar to bar, bragging of their prowess as hunters until the meat spoils and has to be thrown away.

This behavior gives no honor to the hunter or the deer.

---

[11] Make good use of the extra vermouth. Add olives and gin.

A Hunter's Tale

O'er hardwood ridge
thru cedar swamp
I trail the whitetail buck
tho now I fear
'tis my bad luck
I ain't there
he ain't here
So I sit my rump
upon a stump
to smoke my pipe
to contemplate
while down the trail
to my travail
that buck is early
or I am late
With a laugh he blows
and off he goes
into that cedar bog
while I sit here
with a listening ear
like a bump upon a log
Now where he goes
no one knows
I hope he's fairing well
'tis my good luck
he's just a buck
and I've a tale to tell

Today's Hunter

Most of the deer I have shot over the years have been at very close range. The biggest buck I have ever shot was so close that I couldn't tell what part of the deer I was looking at thru the scope--the distance by measure was 30 feet. I have two things that help me get this close, as you soon will see.

Hunting has now become a sport, much like golf or tennis. You need, I am told, the correct clothes and equipment. The more you spend, the better hunter you will be. This type of hunter is not usually from around here.

Hunters now need: a $20,000 4/4 truck, with an ATV and a snowmobile on a trailer, coming along behind; a set of hunting togs that cost more than I ever made in a month of hard work; a rifle that costs more than I needed to support my family with meat for the winter. These guns could drop an elephant.

Bionic ears, walky-talkies so they can talk to each other and who knows how much other gear they think they need to kill a poor deer that doesn't stand much of a chance anyway. These mighty hunters still might go home meatless.

I figure if they were to get real lucky, their meat must run them about $50 a pound. These hunters could bring 100 lbs of lobster with them and it would be cheaper than the deer meat they might not get.

I have maybe shot more deer with a gun costing under $100 than these hunters have shot in their lifetime.

Times to Hunt?

Most hunters put forth the theory that daybreak and the edge of dark are the best times to hunt. The reason for this is so they can return to camp in the middle of the day and do what they do best, which is eat, play cards, and lie a lot. The deer however don't follow this program. They have no sense of fair play at all.

The middle of the day is one of the more active times for deer to be up and about. I have had hunters tell me that deer feed at night and sleep all day and you will have to kick them out of their beds in order to see them at all.

This is not the case. If you wish to know about a deer's habits, watch any cud-chewing animal for 12hrs or so (in the daylight) and you will have a good idea how a deer spends its time.

A deer hardly ever lays down for more than 2 hrs. The need for food is ever present and they must browse almost constantly.

The bucks when in the rut have another drive that keeps them on their feet. They forget to eat and get very little rest during this time. If you only got your loving once a year you would be a little antsy yourself.

Bucks during this period lose weight and stamina and may not make it thru a winter of deep snow and deep cold.

When I went on a hunt, I went to spend the day. The most productive time for me was from 8:00 to 10:00 AM, although I have taken many deer while eating my lunch around noontime.

Ask hunters you know how many times they have seen deer while walking back to camp in the middle of the day.

In my experience there is no best time to hunt although you could say, "the time that you get your deer is the very best time of all.[12]

The Noise Factor

I have heard a lot of hunters over the years say that the reason they didn't get their deer was because the woods were too noisy. Unless you are hunting in the rain or on wet snow the woods are always noisy.

The quietest Native American hunter could not walk silently on a hardwood ridge when the leaves are frozen.

If deer jumped and ran every time they heard a noise in the woods they would be running most of the time. Other deer, moose, bear, and even squirrels make a lot of loud noise when walking on frozen leaves.

The secret is to walk as a deer walks. A deer walks slow and stops often to browse, to test the wind and to listen. If you teach yourself to walk in this way you will see deer standing and even laying down.

The Scent Factor

The deer's nose used to be their greatest weapon for staying alive. Today this is not the case.

Deer have always hated the smell of man for some reason; maybe our deodorant isn't working as well as we would like to think. You have heard, if you have been around hunters or hunt yourself, deer blowing at the hunter. Some hunters believe that only bucks are likely to do this, but does do this also. They do this when we get so close to them that our smell fills their nose and they are trying to blow the scent back out.

Now that we humans have invaded every nook and cranny of what used to be the deer's exclusive domain, they have become rather bored with it all. Farmers and loggers now work almost side by side with the deer. Campers, hikers and fisherman (make that fish-persons) are everywhere at all times. I sometimes wonder if anyone is working for a living anymore. The deer have their noses full of the human scent, exhaust fumes, gas and oil fumes and all the other smells we carry with us. About the only scent that still makes them sit up and pay attention is the smell of dog, although I have gotten very close to deer in the off-season when my dog was with me. Maybe they are becoming bored with this smell as well.

When hunting I use no deodorant, shaving lotion or scented soaps. I don't know if this practice is even necessary anymore.

One thing I know that gets me close to deer and the deer close to me is one of those "doe-in-heat" urine concoctions.

---

[12] I have never shot a deer under a light. If you know what you are doing, there is no need.

The following is just one instance of many that I have had happen that proves, to me at least, how this scent affects deer.

When the blaze-orange law came into effect I, wrongly, I might add, believed that there was no way that I could get close to a deer all lit up like the Las Vegas strip. To get around what I thought at the time was a stupid law designed solely for people who are not from around here, I carried my green hat and coat in a backpack. I would find a place to sit, remove all my orange and don my greens.

On a very cold and windy day I was sitting on a hardwood ridge with the wind in my face and a good field of vision all around. I had removed my legal clothes and replaced them with the greens and had perfumed myself with the before mentioned doe urine. When I became so cold that I could sit no longer I stood up, changed my clothes again and turned around. Six deer were standing there watching me and my performance. How long they had been standing there I do not know, they were so close that whatever scent I was giving off must have been pleasing to them.

I shot the only one with horns as that was the law at the time but the rest of them didn't seem in any hurry to leave so I shot one more for camp meat.

There have been many such instances over the years and I thank Oscar Cronk and his doe urine formula for all the meat on my table thru the years.

I have noticed a lot of hunters use masking scents and then clean and oil their rifles every night, there by defeating the purpose.

Another smell that most hunters I have met think drives deer away is the smell of tobacco. Some hunters won't take their tobacco into the woods with them so as not to be tempted to smoke. I use both cigarettes and a pipe. I go into the woods to enjoy myself and smoking is a big part of the enjoyment. As I am not in the woods for just the taking of the deer, I smoke when I wish to.

The biggest buck that I have ever shot was while I was smoking and he was up close and personal at the time. I have often thought that the deer enjoyed my pipe every bit as much as I did. One half or maybe more of all of the deer I have taken were when I was smoking.

Tracking

Tracking is becoming a lost art; maybe this is because most of the old-time trackers are gone now. It is very important to know at least the basics of tracking if you want to put meat on the table.

A good tracker will use his mind as well as his eyes as much or maybe more as the conditions warrant.

We have all wounded deer from time to time. Even though we are "the William Tell-for-shooters," conditions can send the bullet to a point not aimed at.

Knowing what a deer will do in any given circumstances will help in the tracking. A wounded deer will always travel down hill whenever possible, especially the bucks. A wounded deer will always go to water if there is water to be found anywhere in the area.

If you wound a deer, find the spot where the deer was when you fired and stay there for 1hr., at least if you have patience. When you start on the track, look for blood, not just in the track, but out to the sides as well. If the deer doesn't lie down and stiffen up with in a short distance, you've got a tracking job on your hands.

I have heard hunters say that you can't tell the sex of a deer by the tracks, but this is untrue. Does in their travels will go about anywhere they want to regardless of the terrain. A buck on the other hand will seek out the easy going to get to the same destination. Does urinate in the center of the track-a buck off to the side.

The depth of a track and the imprint of the dewclaws suggest a heavy animal, but not always a buck.

I have noticed that in older bucks the hooves are more rounded at the tip than in younger bucks and does.

Deer are born and spend their entire lives within a three square mile area, this means that they are forever going in circles, much the same as some of us do. Always look to both sides of the track while following your deer. Chances are that this is where your deer will be. Also pay very close attention to any high ground along the sides of the track, as deer like to look down on their back trail. They are usually chuckling to themselves at this time.

There is a lot more about tracking but to cover it all would fill a book. You maybe could find books on tracking at your public library.[13]

Hunting Togs and Boots

There are many man-made fabrics on the market today. Most will keep you warm and dry but are very expensive. One draw back besides the cost is that they are noisy. The noise they make sounds like something walking on the leaves and this keeps your head on a swivel, looking for what is making all that noise.

Woolens on the other hand are quiet. These also keep you warm even when wet. They do however become very heavy.

Cotton long-handle drawers under woolens have been the best combination I have found no matter what the weather or temperature might be.

The boots available today are a vast improvement over the footwear of the good old days. I have found that even though a good pair of boots are costly, they are the best investment you can make to insure a comfortable hunt. Cold or wet feet can ruin your day.

My choice of a hunting boot is one of insulated rubber. They must be light in weight with good support at the ankle and instep. For sub-zero cold I wear felt packs of rubber bottoms and leather uppers. I wear a pair of cotton socks with woolen socks over them. The cotton dries out perspiration. I use back-saver inserts. This helps with leg and back fatigue.

These choices once saved my life at temperatures of 40 and 45 degrees below zero.

---

[13] There is one important thing to remember that all good trackers know: "tracks make poor eating."

Idiots on Ice

One February back in the early sixties, the temperature dropped below zero and stayed there for thirty days. The low for this period was 55 degrees below zero, the highest 30 degrees below zero.

The ice fishing for game fish had just opened and I had heard that the trout were biting at Palmer pond. I called a friend of mine, Johnny Lanctot, to see if he wanted to make the trip in and spend the weekend. He agreed, so we now have two idiots headed for trouble.

This trip would consist of a seven mile skiing jaunt and an over-night camp-out.

We reached the jump-off point just before daybreak after a ride of 30 miles in a truck with no heater. Strapping on our skis, (these nowhere near resembled the skis in use today--we had leather toe straps and inner tube bindings) we shouldered our packs and away we went. The temperature on leaving home was 45 degrees below zero. We arrived at the pond around 10:A.M. and dividing the chores, Johnny started erecting the lean-to and I went in search of firewood.

Walking around the edge of the pond in search of wood I went thru the ice up to my waist. Upon reaching dry land I rolled in the snow (this soaks up water from woolens like a sponge). I then took off my boots and let my stockings freeze solid (this makes a good insulation) which didn't take long at these temperatures (see how I am becoming smarter by the minute?) When my sox were frozen I put my boots back on and headed for the lean-to. As we had no extra clothing with us we decided that the smartest thing we could do was strap on our skis and beat-feet it for the truck, (the truck with no heater.) The trip out took longer than the trip in as I knew that if I started to sweat I would be in very deep DOO DOO. The next worry was dehydration; I have never been so thirsty in my life! The brooks were all frozen down to the beds and eating snow-no matter how much you want to, will kill you!

I had no ill effects from all of this foolishness, except for being very cold and very tired. It was a long trip home and I didn't even have my Alka-Seltzer™ bottle of brandy for moral support.

How to survive in cold weather was another lesson taught to me by those old-timers that I keep bringing up from time to time. I am one of those old-timers now, thanks to them. This cold weather lore saved my bacon more than once! I hope these tips will maybe mean that you will someday be an old-timer too.[14]

Hunting and the Weather

The weather plays a major role in a successful hunt. The deer are in tune with the weather and this dictates what they will be doing and where and when they will be doing it.

Do not depend on those bright young people in the suits on the TV for your weather information, as they are usually wrong 90% of the time. How anyone can hold a job with this kind of record is way beyond me. They have satellites, radar,

---

[14] Insert cuss words where appropriate.

sonar, computers and a crotched stick as tools to perform their job. I think they need to use the crotch stick more often.

They spend hours of airtime telling us why it didn't do what they told us it was going to do the day before.

My uncle Walt could wake up in the morning, gauge the level of pain in his joints, check the corn on his big toe and tell what the weather would be for the next 24 hrs. If he was still with us today, him and me could buy us a couple of suits, go on the TV and get rich.

The best time to hunt has always been for me in the rain. You can glide thru the woods as quiet as a ghost. The deer can't see you, hear you or smell you but when you get close enough you can smell them. Their wet hide gives off an odor much the same as any animal when wet. I think everyone has known the odor of a wet dog or horse.

I have walked right up to deer when it was raining, that were sound asleep, curled up in a ball and laying right out in the open with no cover to hide them. Once while hunting in a heavy rain I climbed up on a blow-down to get a better look at the area, when I jumped down I landed on a deer that was sound asleep on the other side. There was a great explosion of wet deer and wet hunter. I don't think my heart slowed down for the rest day.

The moral of this story is: LOOK BEFORE YOU LEAP.

When I was young and full of myself, snow was my next best time to hunt. I would find a fresh track first thing in the morning (usually by flashlight.) I would then start on the track, walking 20 paces and trotting 20 paces. At times I could hear the deer up ahead of me but I paid no mind to this. I would just keep pushing the deer as hard as I could.

The whitetail deer has no stamina over the long haul. They are very fast for short distances but they need to stop and blow before they have covered much ground. Usually by noon or shortly after, I would come upon my deer standing with its legs splayed out, its head down with its tongue hanging out. The deer at this time has no idea that I am anywhere around. I would be almost as fresh as when I had started on the track. One shot at a standing deer and it was mine. I used to call this insanity fun. Today I do my best work from the comfort of a hot seat and let the deer come to me.

Deer know when a storm is coming and they will become very active just before the storm arrives. This is a good time to find a stand and spend as much time as your patience will allow. Once the storm has arrived the deer will not move until hunger forces them to and then they do not move very far.

If you pay attention to the animals and birds they can tell you when a storm is on the way. If your potatoes boil dry while cooking it is a sure thing that it will storm in the next 24 hrs. If you are as old as I am your joints will warm you of a coming storm.

Shelters

"Well, here you are!!" you say to yourself. It's late in the day and you are far from home. You have screwed up![15] Maybe you've been tracking a big buck and lost all track of time and place, or maybe as we like to say up here Maine, you got yourself turned around. Whatever the reason you are now looking forward to a long walk in the dark or a night in the woods. The first option can be very tiring and painful; the second, if done right, can be a pleasure.

Are you carrying the things with you that I recommended back a ways? If you are this can be a great experience and a tale to tell. If not, it can be an ordeal.

If the weather is good the sky makes a great roof and the view is breath taking. A windbreak and a reflector for your fire is all that is needed. A blow down that has fallen roots and all serves both of these purposes. If more is needed or if the weather is bad, the next best and easiest shelter is a fir, spruce, or pine tree with limbs almost to the ground. The lower limbs will be dead and can be used for a smokeless fire.

If it is raining, cut fir boughs and weave them into the branches of your tree to make a quick and easy roof. If you can find a flat rock for a reflector for your fire you will keep warm and dry for the night.[16]

Cut some fir bough tips for a bed--you won't be sleeping much as you will be adding wood to your fire all night. You will however get more rest while lying down than sitting up and the boughs will insulate you from the ground.

The third shelter, and the one that requires the most work, is the lean-to. Cut a ridgepole that will span the limbs of two trees about five or six feet apart. Cut fir or spruce saplings about seven to eight feet long and lean them on the ridgepole. Remove the limbs from the under side and weave them into the roof. You will have an almost drip free shelter.

With your shelter secure, your fire going, some raisins for supper and a nip from the ever trusty Alka-Seltzer™ bottle you may find a peace and contentment you never knew existed.

A Hand Gun on a Deer Hunt

The right hand gun can be a useful tool on a deer hunt. However, hunters who tote a large caliber hand gun are carrying around extra weight for no reason that I can figure out unless they think that they will be attacked by something or someone. I call this the John Wayne syndrome. This type of hunter is also usually carrying enough ammo to defeat most Third World countries.

---

[15] I used to plan these screw-ups from time to time just for the adventure of it.

[16] A folded pack of aluminum foil is easy to carry and stretched between two green hardwood sticks makes a great reflector.

As soon as I could afford one I purchased a Ruger 22 automatic. I don't remember when this was but I paid $49.95 for it new if that helps to date this purchase. With a hand gun of this caliber you can carry enough ammo for a hunt without adding much weight.

The 22 hand gun can be used for signaling. I never used mine for this purpose, maybe there were a few times when I should have but my pride wouldn't let me. There was however a few nights that I spent in the woods when this little hand gun put a rabbit or a partridge or both on my spit. With the afore mentioned raisins for dessert and my Alka-Seltzer™ bottle of brandy I enjoyed a meal fit for a king.

I have shot many a partridge for the pot with this little 22 while deer hunting and I would like to say that this does not scare away the deer.

I shot a partridge on the edge of a chopping one morning and while dressing it out, looked up to see a spike-horn buck watching me like he had bought a ticket and was going to stay until the show was over, but needless to say, you know where he ended up.

Gun shots do not scare deer! More than once I have shot a deer out of a bunch and have had the rest of them stand there just begging me to break the law and sometimes I did.

I have since up-graded my hand gun to a Ruger stainless steel automatic with a bull barrel, target grips and target sights. This is by far the most accurate hand gun I have ever owned. I couldn't begin to count the birds that I have put in the pot with this side-arm.

The Deer Gun

I wish that I could tell you here what is the ideal gun, however there is no such animal. The deer gun that fits you and shoots where you point it: that's the ideal deer gun for you.

I shot my first deer with a single shot Stevens 22. My father bought out a punchboard for $11.00 just to get the rifle. He also got 24 boxes of chocolates. I made out like a bandit on that deal. With this first rifle, I shot rabbits, partridge and the one deer. I never had the courage to try for bear or moose with so little firepower.

Who knows what a punchboard is? As I mentioned before, my Grand Dad was a professional hunter. He used a 44-40 Winchester carbine. He used this for small game as well as deer, bear and moose. Later on he saved his pennies and traded for a 30-by-God-30 Winchester rifle. It cost him the unheard of sum of $7.00. Grand Dad was blind in his right eye so he shortened the stocks on his guns so that he could shoot with his left eye off his right shoulder.

My first deer rifle was a 30-30 Winchester model 94. Back then this was considered by most to be the ideal choice in a deer gun. The thinking was that you needed a good brush gun.[17] I picked the 30-30 because of the low price and all the cowboys in the movies used them.

---

[17] Why anyone would wish to shoot brush I will never know.

The 12 gauge shotgun with slugs or buckshot or both was also considered a good brush gun and if you are hunting brush I recommend it highly.

With all the clear-cutting going on in the Maine woods, I would suggest a rifle that can reach out and touch your game. Even though you might be hunting thick woods you can come to one of these clear-cuts at anytime. I missed seven deer in a bunch at Kelly Brook after the clear-cutting started because I didn't have enough gun to reach them. I tried but I stretched the barrel on that little 30-30 so far that it never was the same after that shot.

Most of my deer have been shot at very close range (I'm talking feet not yards here), yet I still prefer a flat shooting, hard-hitting caliber.

I have always had a love affair with firearms. If I could afford it I would have a house full. I used to buy, sell and trade guns as a hobby. This was not a good thing. Hunting with so many different guns results in missed deer. Some of these guns were good, some not so good. Experience has taught me to find the right gun and stick to it. I have owned guns that cost very little and have found them to be up to the job. I have owned guns that cost quite a bit of money that weren't worth lugging on a hunt.

Figure 10: Bub packing in for a fall bird hunt.

Some of these guns were so heavy you needed wheels to haul them through the woods.

The last few years of my hunting, I used a custom made 30-06 with souped-up hand loads. This featherweight rifle was easy to carry and I think the most accurate rifle that I have ever owned.

Trying to tell you what deer rifle you should own would be like telling a Chevy owner to buy a Ford.

If you find a rifle that feels right and fits you, if it is accurate and has the stopping power, *this is your ideal deer gun.*

Happy Hunting

The Old Family Deer Gun

This old gun of mine
A long ways back in time
It was a gun so fine
It's not so fine anymore
It's now become a smooth-bore

Now it's not so good I fear
I aim it over there
The shot goes over here

I fired it once this year
And with any luck at all
That shot will become my deer
Sometime next fall

One Night in the Woods

The storm was a heavy wet snow. It started about 3:00 AM. I left camp before first light and with my flashlight I started up the brook looking for a fresh track. I hadn't gone very far when I came across the track of a nice sized buck. He had came down off the ridge and gone into the swamp. I just knew that he was a little ways into the swamp and would be lying down after his night of courtship. As soon as I could see the track without the light, I started on his trail. I hadn't gone far when I could smell the odor steaming from his wet hide. I guess he could smell the odor coming off my wet hide also because he went out of the swamp and back up over the ridge. I followed him up the ridge and down the ridge until noon, never seeing or hearing him but getting a whiff of him from time to time. We are both sweating up an odor by now. We had returned to our starting point and he had gone back into the swamp again.

I sat down and had my lunch and a pipe and debated if I should stay on him for a awhile longer or let him go. I opt for a couple more hours, he must be getting tired by now, going up and down that ridge, I know I was.

The next thing I know it is dark and snowing hard. Now I have a decision to make: a long wet walk in the snow and the dark or a night in the woods.

The wood stove, a few hot buttered rums, and a warm sleeping bag back at camp make this look very inviting but I am not sure just where I am, the snow storm makes everything look different to me. I can find my way back by compass but this will be a long slow process. The night will be half gone by the time I can find the camp. I opt for the night in the woods. Its not too cold so I know if I can get dried out a little bit I will be just fine.

Just before it got dark I had come thru a stand of fir trees with ledges scattered thru them. This will furnish me with all the comforts I will need to see me thru the night. On backtracking to the grove of fir I found a ledge a little taller than I am, this gives me a wall for my shelter and a reflector for my fire. A fire is my first need to give me some light to work by. I scouted around until I found a fir blow-down. This would give me tinder and dry small wood to start my fire. While trimming limbs from the under side, I came across an abandoned squirrels nest. This is the best fire starter you can find. I will not need my candle to start this fire. After bringing all of this to my rock I had to find bigger wood to keep my fire going. Three or four trips and I now can start my fire.

Next I select six small firs 8-10 feet in length and remove the limbs from one side. I lean these up against the rock and I now have a wall and a roof. The boughs that I have trimmed make my bed.

In just a little while over an hour I am ready to set up housekeeping. I made a clothes line with my parachute cord and a few crotched sticks and hung my coat up to dry. It is now time for a nip from the Alka-Seltzer™ bottle and a pipe. At times like this I wish that Alka-Seltzer™ came in bigger bottles.

My supper is raisins washed down with the rest of my brandy. Adding wood to the fire I stoke up my pipe, sit back and contemplate just how little you need in this life to be totally happy.

There is not a sound to be heard, the woods are still except for falling snowflakes and the flicker of the fire. If there is a God I am now sitting at his or her right hand. I am not a religious man but this is an experience that will make you become one, at least for a little while.

When my coat is dry I hang my shirts in its place and put the coat back on.

This night passes much too fast. I catnap off and on thru the night adding wood to the fire every once and again. When the sky starts turning grey I reluctantly leave my little home and make my way back to camp and breakfast.

I have never feared the woods at night and if I had to I could have survived for many days and nights just by keeping my firewood replenished and taking any game I came across in the area.

If I could find some way to keep my Alka-Seltzer™ bottle full of brandy I would be a very happy man.

Getting the Big Bucks

Most everyone who gets a big buck brags on this feat. I am as guilty of this as anyone. Why this is so I cannot say. Some of these people feel that they must write of their exploits, I am now guilty of this also. In reading these stories I have found that as human comedies they read very well. As a way to get your buck, most are a joke.

One hunter claimed that if you go into the area that you plan to hunt in September and study the habits of the bucks, you would be able to pick a spot for your stand where the deer are feeding. This hunter claimed that this is almost as good as having your buck tied to a tree waiting for you on opening day.

If you follow this advice, I wish you "lots of luck." I wish that deer were this obliging, however deer don't play the game by these rules.

Where and what the deer are eating in early fall is not what they will be eating come hunting season. These early foods have gone by later in the fall when you will be hunting. The routes they take to and from feeding areas will change also.

It is also said that watching scrapes will bag the big bucks. I have found this to be a waste of time. Bucks make these scrapes on all four sides of their territory-which is not a lot of ground for them to cover but quite a hike for us. The buck paws the ground bare to make his scrape-always under a small evergreen tree-urinates on it and then places a front hoof print on the scrape. This tells all other bucks that the does within the area belong to HIM. It takes three days for him to complete his rounds. Usually his visits are nocturnal so sitting on one of these scrapes is nothing more than a crapshoot.

About 80% of the deer I have taken over the years have been bucks. The reason for this is simple--they are the only guys in the woods dumber than me. When they come into the rut their necks swell up, their eyes glaze over and become red. They get a fire in their belly that controls their actions all during this period. They go charging in where angels fear to tread. If they ever had any sense to begin with it is now gone. Food and rest are nothing, "loving is everything."

Keep hunting in the area that bucks are working; a few drops of doe-in-heat urine, patience and staying alert should produce a buck for you. If you have mastered the use of the deer call, this will increase the odds in your favor also.

I will have some buck stories to tell later on in the book, none of which will be depicting me as anything more than a good hunter with a lot of luck.

Deer do not have strategies to outsmart us hunters. They have instincts and habits and these you need to know. You can't outwit a witless animal.

I have called deer to me with a deer-call of my own making. I was shown how to do this by one of those old-timers I keep telling you about. I don't know to this day if I am actually calling them or the noise just peaks their curiosity.

The more time spent where the deer live and the more you know about their habits should make for a successful hunt.

GOOD HUNTING

Figure 11: The author and an 11-point buck.

Story of the Deer Call

Back in the late fifties, on a warm fall day (deer season opened in October,) I was a long way back in the big woods of northwestern Maine. This was all new country for me so I was exploring as much as I was hunting. Come noon I found myself high up on the side of a mountain. There was a good view of the country so I stopped here under a big pine tree to have my lunch. I had finished my sandwich and was enjoying a pipe when I saw one of them "old-timers" coming up the ridge towards me. This was a surprise since I thought that I was all alone in my little corner of the world. I invited him to sit a spell as I saw a chance here to maybe further my education. I had another pipe and he had a chew of tobacco and I asked him where he was from. Turned out he had a cabin just over the mountain and lived there year round. He made his living from trapping, hunting and fishing and only left the woods to sell his furs and buy supplies.

He had an object hanging around his neck so I had to ask him what it was. He told me it was his deer-call. He showed me how he made it and how to use it. I asked him how he knew the call to make on it, as I had never heard deer make much talk amongst themselves. "Goats," he says, "study goats." I will now try to pass his wisdom on to you.

The thing you will need most to make your deer call is a lot of patience and not too much of your favorite beverage. The cost is the price of the rawhide and the elastic band.

Deer are not a talkative bunch so this is where the goats come into the process. The old-timer told me that the only domestic animal that talks like a deer is a goat.

Now not wanting to spend a whole lot of time hanging around goats, I took a tape recorder to a fellow I knew who raised goats. I asked him if he had any nannies that were in the mood for loving and if he did could I record her while she was telling the world all about it. Playing this tape enabled me to practice with my call until I got it right.

To make your call you will need a piece of cedar about 1 inch in diameter and about 4 inches long. A 3ft. length of rawhide bootlace and a rubber band ¼ inch wide. The cedar must be green and smooth.

Remove the bark and with a saw cut the cedar lengthwise down the middle. On each half remove some of the wood in the center of the two pieces about 1½ inch long and 1/8 inch deep, tapering to nothing at the ends.

If you can excuse my bad drawing, it should now look like this.

Figure 12: Hole in the deer call.

While you are doing all of this, soak the rawhide in water until it is fully saturated.

Cut a notch around each end of the call the width and depth of the rawhide.

Place the elastic band the length of ½ of the call and put the two pieces together. Hold the ends tight together with your fingers and with the goat tape playing, pull on one end of the elastic band-, blowing thru the call until you get the same tone and pitch as the tape. (If you own a goat omit the tape). You might have to deepen or lengthen the center hole to achieve this. You also might have to carve a whole new piece of cedar if you have cut too long and deep.

This is where the patience comes into the picture. I have carved as many as 10 calls before I had one that I was happy with.

Blow thru both sides of the call as each side will give you a different sound. When you have the sound you are looking for, mark the elastic band so you can keep the same tension when you secure the two pieces with the rawhide.

When you have determined the correct side of the call, carve a V on both sides with the point of the V away from you, the open end of the V will be the side that you blow into.

Cut a piece of the wet rawhide long enough to tie one end of the call together. With your elastic band set to the mark, tie the other end with the long piece of rawhide that you have left over. Make a loop so to be able to wear the call around your neck. The reason for this is that it takes less movement than it does to dig around in your pockets trying to find it.

Your deer call should look like this if you have done the job right.

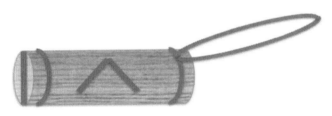

Figure 13: Finished deer call.

Do not imbibe too much of your favorite beverage while making your deer call. It may produce a sound that will drive the deer into the next county.

If you can now sing like a horny goat and have done everything right, buy some insurance against being trampled by crazed bucks.

Figure 14: Gerry Savage and his son "Sure-shot" with his first deer, thereby the nickname. His age here is 14 and he is very proud.

Figure 15: On the left, my son Dave, his 8-point buck and on the right, me.

So You Got Lucky: Care and Preparation

We haven't enjoyed a beverage for quite a spell so before reading on you might wish to knock back a few.

You have pulled the trigger and the adrenalin has receded back to normal, you are now at the time when fun's over. The hard work can now begin.

If you want tender meat without that gamey taste people are always talking about, what you do from this moment on becomes very important.

I have never had tough or gamey meat from any deer that I have prepared from the first step to the last, the last being the total enjoyment of the results of the hunt.

I was taught by the old-timers that the first thing to do is bleed out the animal. I have found that this does not need to be done. I think this belief stems from the killing of cattle and hogs where this has been and still is the practice.

The first thing to do with a male deer is remove the sex organs (after making sure that the spirit of the animal has departed) as soon as possible as they will taint the meat of the hindquarters and the tender loins. If the deer is a doe and is not barren, you need to remove the milk sack. Try to keep this intact and remove as a unit.

The next step is to position your deer so that the stomach is lower than the backbone. Spread the hind legs (this is where the before mentioned parachute cord comes in handy). With your small lock-back knife make a shallow cut from the crotch to the ribs. I put two fingers under the back of the blade to control the depth of the cut. Should you cut too deep the aroma will make this job very unpleasant. If you have done everything right so far the paunch will slide out almost by itself. Pull the deer away from this mess so that you will have a clean place to work.

Cut a hardwood sapling with your belt knife about a foot long and ¼ inch in diameter. Make a cut just thru the hide around the anus and pull; this will remove most of the poop tube (notice these technical terms). Push the sapling you have cut thru the canal to remove any material left inside.

Pull out the lungs and sever the windpipe. Pick up the front of the deer to drain any remaining blood left in the body cavity. If there is water handy I wash out the body cavity at this time.

If I am alone and intend to get the deer back to camp the same day I leave the heart and liver attached. This allows me to have both hands free for dragging the deer.

As soon as possible hang the deer by the back legs with a spreader to keep the legs apart. If the weather is cool enough and it is possible, the hide should be removed at this time. The skinning process is much easier while there is still some body heat left in the animal.

Salt and pepper any bullet holes or cuts in the meat. If it is warm enough for flies to be up and about, wrap the entire animal with cheesecloth. This will keep the flies from laying eggs in the meat. Once this is done, let the carcass hang for from 3-4 weeks. If it is too warm to do this and you do not have access to a walk-in cooler this may not be possible.

I purchased a used fridge for $25.00. This allows me to age my meat in warm weather. By removing shelves and the use of a spring-loaded closet rod I am able to quarter my deer and hang it inside.

When I was a young tad back on the farm we had no electricity. All the meat we had for the winter was hung in the wood shed. The meat would change color from red to brown to black. The longer the meat hung the better it tasted. When the meat froze my dad used a hatchet to cut junks of meat from the carcass.

I cut and wrap my own deer and it is a very simple process. The back loins that would be the chops I remove from the bone just by getting my fingers between the backbone and the meat and pull.

I slice these into steaks ¼ inches thick except for one roast that is mentioned in the stuffing recipe.

The tenderloins in the average deer are only about 8-10 inches long and about as big around as a half dollar. I slice these ½ inch thick and eat them "right now."

Probing with your fingers until you find the seams between the sections of meat can separate the different cuts from the rear quarters. Once these are removed, slice to desired thickness and wrap. I like my deer steak about ½ inch thick.

I seem to be all out of tips, there are maybe more but I can't recollect any right now. I hope that the tips I have passed on to you will be of help on your next hunt.

I would like at this time to pass on a story from one of the leading outdoor magazines. I do this to show how not to conduct a deer hunt. It contains all of the things that can ruin what should have been a successful and enjoyable experience.

I will not embarrass the author or the magazine anymore than they have been already by using names.

The Great Maine Horn Hunt
(Or: Horns Make Thin Soup)

Once upon a time there was this famous horn hunter, (he was not from around here) who had shot trophy deer all over the North American continent except Maine. He claimed to have records in "Boone & Crocket" and I guess "Funk & Wagnall's" and the "Encyclopedia Britannica."

Hearing of the hat rack bucks that supposedly lived up here in Maine, he rounds up his hunting buddies, (they by the way are not from around here either), and they head for the north Maine woods. These expert hunters rented a deer camp and not needing to hire a guide, as they knew more about hunting than the average bear, are off on the hunt.

The first morning, feeling that just because the deer camp was located in the middle of the woods, no self-respecting buck would be caught dead in this area-our mighty hunter drives 7 or 8 miles from the camp on a logging road. At this point (or maybe by second sight) it is established that this is where the Big Buck lives.

About this time it starts to snow. Out of the truck and into the woods he goes. There is no mention of a compass in this story, but if there is one, now is the time to use it.

Off he goes with not a clue to the direction he is going or in what direction he will need to go to return to the road where his truck is parked.

No more does he enter the woods when he jumps the Granddaddy of all big bucks. This buck is so big that it is guaranteed to get him into Sears & Roebuck and most any other book with two names in the title.

Off on the track our intrepid hunter goes. The snow has now become an old fashion Maine Nor'easter. He cannot see the end of his gun barrel but he endeavors to persevere (the only way I could track a deer under these conditions would be to hang on to his tail.) All day long our hero tracks this magnificent animal and at three o-clock in the afternoon he spots his prey (it seems he has thought to bring a watch.)

"BANG!" The shot is fired; the trophy is down. What to do now? It is getting dark and at this point we find that our hunter has no knife. He cannot dress his deer and this is the least of his problems. No knife; no compass; no matches; no lunch. And in a strange woods with not the foggiest idea where he is.

Wanting to find his trophy buck should he get himself out of the woods and find his way back again, he lays a rifle shell on the deer carcass figuring he will be able to see this when he returns; "lots of luck."

Picking a direction by a system known only to him, perhaps by a coin toss, he starts what will be a very long wet walk.

This has to be the luckiest man alive. After walking all night he finds another logging road and is picked up by a woodsman on his way to work, who gives him a ride to his truck.

On reaching camp he regales his buddies with tales of his hunting prowess and his knowledge of woods lore. He now enlists their help in searching for a rifle shell buried under a foot of snow. Needless to say, the rifle shell and the deer are still there.

A belt knife to put blaze marks on the backs of the trees as he left the woods would have led him back to his buck. This is presuming he knew what woods he was in or what direction he needed to go in to find the blaze marks. How a man can call himself an expert hunter and commit this comedy of errors is way beyond me. This hunter should have had his trophy deer, a night in the woods with heart and liver for his supper and a really great story to tell.

Buck Fever

Buck fever is a phenomenon I have heard about from the time I started hunting. I took all of these stories with a grain of salt. Nobody to my way of thinking could act as foolish as these stories indicated. If these stories were true, I felt that no way could something like this happen to me. Well, was I ever wrong!

One of these stories starts with my quest for the ideal bird gun; I had been pestering my dad for a shotgun that could shoot more than one shot at a time. I was coming home with less birds than I felt I could bag if I had a repeating shotgun or at least a side by side. My little 22 single shot was not getting the job done.

My Dad had this pal (he was also his boss) who was an avid duck hunter. One Saturday, this friend of my Dad's showed up at the house with a brand new J.C. Higgens 12. ga. pump shotgun with a 30 inch barrel. This was the ideal duck gun. Out to the backfield they go with the new duck gun and a six-pack of their favorite beverage to do some wing shooting. "We are now trying out the new shotgun."

After much shooting and bragging and one more six-pack, it was decided to load up the car and go find a deer.

Just before you came into the village of Athens, there was a field with some apple trees in the middle of it. (There is a church there now). When these two intrepid hunters came around the corner, low and behold, there stands a buck eating apples and, in general, minding his own business.

The owner of this brand-spanking new duck gun proceeds to cram it full of shells (it held five shots). Out of the car he goes, across the road and into field yelling "BANG" at the top of his lungs and pumping out a shell at every yell. My dad walked along behind picking up the shells and putting them in his pocket.

About this time, the buck, having eaten his fill of apples and getting just a little fed-up with all this foolishness and goings on walks off into the woods.

Back to the car go the mighty hunters. There is not much said for a few miles down the road. A few beverages were consumed. My dad says, "that ain't much of a gun you have got there." The owner says, "I think you're right, do you want to buy it?" A ways down the road and a beverage or two later, Dad says, "my boy wants a new shotgun, I might take it off your hands if the price is right."

For $35.00 I had me a new shotgun that didn't shoot so good.

Buck Fever Tale #2

Once upon a time, there was this friend of ours who was an old-time poacher from the old school. He couldn't shoot a deer unless it was under a light. I do not condone this practice, but you know who you know.

One day we talked this fella with the night vision to go hunting with us in the daylight. He hunted with a 303 British rifle. He carried two clips of ammo so he was always loaded for bear.

On our way to the area we were going to hunt, a young buck stepped into the road in front of us. As our boy was riding shotgun, we expected him to shoot the deer. He just sat there so we both yelled, "shoot that buck!"

It must have been the daylight that messed him up because he proceeded to unload all of his clips, put the shells in his pocket and then claim that he had no shells for his rifle.

If he was alive today he would deny that this ever happened.

Now that I have laid the foundation for this sort of foolishness, it is now my turn. I am the hunter that this could never happen to. With a lifetime of hunting, being taught by the best, I am the cool calm and collected hunter.

Buck Fever Tale #2: A Sorry Tale

This story takes place at Kelly Brook. Who would have guessed?

As has been mentioned before, I have shot many a large buck in this area, so many in fact that it seemed to be an easy thing to do.

On this day, the second day of our hunt, I had been out since before daylight. Signs were plentiful and I knew where the big bucks lived.

Come noon I was about middle way up a hardwood ridge. Below me was mixed growth of mostly scrub fir.

I had finished my lunch and was enjoying a pipe, letting my mind wander and taking advantage of one of those quiet times that are so special to a hunter. Down the ridge in the scrub growth I saw a deer get up out of its bed. Once it was on its feet the only part of the deer that I could see was legs.

Being one of those hunters who know everything, I knew that this deer was going to head down the ridge to the brook for a drink. I will not most likely ever see this deer again, at least not on this day.

Smoking my pipe and cursing the nature of things in general, I look up to the biggest rack of horns I have ever seen and they are coming right at me. Not wanting to chance missing this deer I decide to wait for a body shot. While waiting I now start counting the points, the total comes to 24.

There is no way that I am going to get a shot at this deer. He is too big, he is too smart, he knows I am here, he is going to change course and leave me with my bare face hanging out, this I know.

He keeps coming and I now see this big brown eye, it looks big as a pie plate. My left leg starts to shake. I do not want to lose this deer. He is the highlight of all my years of hunting.

I am using my son's 30-by-God-30 saddle-ring carbine, why, I forget.

Watching this majestic animal, I stand up and proceed to load shells into a gun that is already loaded. The words I use at this time cannot be repeated in mixed company. This gun is broke. The deer is still coming. Now I can see the neck. I have no idea what to do next. I am thinking that maybe I can cut his throat with my belt knife.

I am thinking of all the guns that I have owned that worked. I am thinking, why I left my rifle back at the camp.

The deer is still coming closer. I am in a state of total confusion.

When the deer finally emerges from the fir scrub he is all of 10 feet from me in all of his magnificence. I have never seen such an animal.

Now both legs are shaking and here I am with a rifle in one hand, a hand full of shells in the other and I do not have a clue what to do next. A club would have done this deer in.

For some reason my senses now return to me. The guns not broke after all. I need to do something even if it's wrong. From the hip I empty the gun as fast as I can lever it and pull the trigger. This might look good in the movies or on TV, but I shot the tops off of a lot of trees.

This buck, becoming bored with it all, walked off and left me with an empty gun and the air turning blue from my now extended cussing vocabulary.

I wish him well and many does.

Bubbu's Big Buck
(Or: Who Does the Dishes)

As I always was appointed camp cook I was exempt from dish washing and other camp chores. The artful dodging when it came to decide who the dish washer would be was usually done by some form of gambling.

Bubba's method of deer hunting

Bub believed that when it was time for him to get his deer, it would just happen with out too much effort on his part. How he determined this time or where this miracle would happen was never revealed. He had stated many times that he could stay in his bunk and his deer would crawl in bed with him, kiss him on the lips and ask to be put in the frying pan.

On this weeks hunt, Bub, my son Dave and yours truly were at the camp. My son was 11 years old at the time. I took him out of school for 1 week every fall from the time he was 10.

The usual debate on who would be doing the dishes started almost as soon as we arrived at camp.

After opening up the camp, stowing the supplies and our gear, we sat down to the table to consummate the "opening the camp" ritual.

After several beverages, Bub made the brag that who every bagged the first deer would not have to do dishes all week. My son Dave, knowing how Bub conducted his deer hunts figured that this bet was a sure thing, agreed.

Monday morning Dave and me left camp before daylight. Bub was still in the rack. About 9:30, nature's call requires that he arise. Taking his 32-40 he walked out back a short distance, answered nature's call and shot his biggest buck.

As Bub believes that pulling the trigger is doing his part, when we arrived a couple of hours later, he was sitting on a stump, smoking his pipe, waiting for me to perform the surgery.

Bubba will do anything to get out of doing the dishes.

I have quite a few big buck stories and of does as well. Most of them, if you have read one you have read them all. This next story I am about to tell is of the biggest buck of my hunting career, the one that did not get away.

I am not claiming any special expertise in the taking of this trophy deer. In fact, most of what I know about deer and hunting seemed to desert me at the crucial moment. I guess that is why I am adding it to the book.

This will be a very long-winded story so you will maybe want to lay in a supply of a favorite beverage and some junk food.

Figure 16: Bub with one of his nice bucks taken at Kelly Brook

Up Close and Personal

This trophy buck came to me in the fall of 1969. I was working construction at the time as a foreman. The job was winding down and lay offs were expected. I knew that I wasn't on the lay off list but with my devious mind I contrived to get my self on it as deer season was just around the corner. I was one of two foremen to be picked for promotion to general foreman, the other to work with his tools until a transfer to a new job. Being the nice guy that I am I dropped out of the running. I also convinced my boss that a month's deer hunting would make a new man of me and I could come back in December and lick the world with one hand. After a lot of crying in my beer I finally weaseled my way to a pink slip.

I couldn't sign up for my rocking chair money until Monday morning so I spent the weekend pacifying the wife and packing and repacking my gear.

Monday morning I was at the office of the idle rich as soon as the doors opened. First in line I signed for my checks and headed north for Kelly Brook camp.

It was late afternoon by the time I had made two backbreaking trips into camp and stowed all my gear. Too late and too tuckered out to hunt I swamped out the camp, moved the mice to new homes and enjoyed a few beverages.

The next morning the temperature was at the 0 degree mark and being in no hurry to freeze my extremities, I left camp after the sun had come up and warmed things up just a tad.

I have to take just a minute here to talk about rifles as they play a big part in this tale.

That year I had traded for a 308 Winchester automatic with a scope. Soon after I got the thing I decided I did not like it much. Not being able to afford a swap, I was stuck with it. Along with this rifle, I took my son's 30-30 Winchester saddle-ring carbine. This rifle was made in 1909 and looking down the barrel, one could see the age of this weapon.

Figuring on this first day to be looking over the area in preparation for some serious hunting, I took my boy's gun and left the "I don't like the 308" on the rack.

With my pockets full of what was needed for a day and maybe a nights time in the woods, a few drops of doe urine on my hat and my deer call that I had spent all fall working on until it sounded like a horny goat, I ventured forth in search of the elusive whitetail.

As soon as I crossed the brook I knew I was in for a very noisy day. The trees were snapping with the cold, were there was mud there was upside down icicles. Walking in the leaves was a good imitation of a herd of elephants. I now give a couple of blats on my deer call, the theory being that any deer on the ridge will think that I am one of them.

Not wanting to make a lot of noise right yet, I decide to light up a Camel, which by the way I had not a walked a mile for yet. I had no more than fired up my smoke when I hear something coming down the ridge making so much noise I just know it has to be a moose. Right now I am not too excited. By the time I had finished my smoke I was looking at the biggest buck I had ever seen in all my years of roaming the Maine woods. As it looked like he wished to be in the same place as I was, I watched him come closer and closer. Now the adrenalin is starting to build and I just know he will sense that I am here and take himself back up the ridge. I now think that if I am going to shoot, it had better be now. The first shot that I fire, breaks off a small tree that I never saw was there. All I was seeing was that big buck. The deer is still standing there, chewing his cud and getting a good whiff of doe urine. I am now so excited that I have no idea were my next shot went. Now this buck wants nothing more to do with me anymore and takes himself back up over the ridge and out of sight.

Turning the air blue with colorful cussing, I decide to see if I can find some camp meat. My heart is not in this. My mind is on that trophy buck.

At noon I return to camp with no camp meat and no buck hanging on the game pole. As I was planning to spend most of a month at camp, this is not a good thing.

In need of a plan to get a chance at this buck that is growing in my mind by the minute, I now try to become smarter than the average deer. I know that in the later afternoon the deer come to the brook to drink, but it is a long brook. Where to be that is the question? There is a blow down on the ridge at the edge of a cutting that gives a good view of the ridge and of the brook for quite a distance. I have sat on this many a time, as it is very comfortable. I have fell asleep on it many times as well.

I take myself up to the blow down about 3:00 that afternoon and get settled in. This time I have the 308; there will be no more of the shooting of trees on this hunt.

Two blats on the deer call as this seemed to work very well that morning and a drop or two of the doe urine and I am ready. I know that buck has my name written all over him.

About 3:30 it is starting to get dark. I decide one more blat on the call and a smoke and by then it will be time to head back for camp (I have now walked a mile for my Camel.) Here comes that moose again only this time I know better. When I finally see him I know he is my friend of the morning fiasco, giving me a second chance (I told you my name was written all over him.) He will not thumb his nose at me again. There will be no more premature shooting. I will wait until he is so close I can kiss him. If he keeps coming towards me, as he seems to want to do, he is on a heading that will put him right in my lap.

This time I am cool calm and collected. I put out my smoke, ease off the safety and ever so slowly raise the rifle. By this time he is so close that I cannot tell what part of the deer the scope is on. I scan towards the front of the deer to see and then up. I am looking into the biggest eye that I have ever seen and his ear.

This is the shot that I have to take. All of this time I am talking to myself, slow movements-easy on the trigger-one shot at the base of the ear and this deer is mine (all of this, with a gun that I don't much like at all.)

The deer is laying 30 feet from me and it is now time for another smoke and a shot from the all-important Alka-Seltzer™ bottle.

After dressing my buck I thought I maybe could drag him down to the brook and wash him out. One tug and I knew that this deer was going nowhere until the boys came in and I could get some help.

This was one of those times when listening to those old-timers paid off. I removed my shirt and under shirt and laid them on the deer. Then I urinated on them; in fact I stayed there until I could do this twice, which between the cold and the excitement was not a very hard thing to do. I was taking no chances of a varmint eating my trophy buck. The heart and liver went back to camp with me and I had my camp meat.

When the boys came in it took four of us to hang him in a tree to keep until I went out for supplies. This was one deer that I intended to tag.

This was the only deer that I ever had weighed. After 11 days of drying out and without the heart and live, he topped out at 287 lbs.

I wish that I had a picture of this deer but we had a fire at one of our other camps ad all the pictures and the horns were lost.

This buck had only 8 points but where they came out of his head they were as big around as my arm.[18]

And therein, lies a tale…

---

[18] This was some of the finest eating of all the deer that I have ever taken.

Figure 17: Working harder getting the Scout to the deer than getting the deer to the Scout

Bow Hunting

I never was a very serious bow hunter. It was just another excuse to get out into the woods.

I have only shot two deer with a bow; both were camp meat and went untagged. I did not want to ruin my firearms' season, as this was my favorite time of the year. I found nothing very challenging to taking a deer this way and if I had to, I feel that I could take a deer this way anytime I needed meat.

I had none of the equipment that is on the market today. I made my own bow from a piece of hornbeam and store-bought arrows. A piece of leather served to protect my forearm and an old glove to protect the fingers of my shooting hand.

It was usually warm during bow season so I wore jeans, moccasins and any shirt that I happen to put on for the day.

There is more "techno-crap" used in bow hunting today than it took to put a man on the moon.

The bow hunter of today looks like, "Rambo" He wears camouflage clothes and paints his face and then climbs a tree where the deer cannot see him anyway.

Deer never look up. They have no natural enemies above them. Some of these hunters have tree stands that can take them up a tree like an elevator.

To me, all of this takes the fun out of what I used to think was something special.

The same principals that apply to firearm hunting also apply to bow hunting. You cannot hide from a deer unless you are up a tree so play on their weakness, "their curiosity.

I have never found any honor in shooting a deer from a tree.

Kelly Brook: The Outlaw Years

A Career Move

I once thought that I would like to become a Maine game warden. As I knew the fields, woods and streams of Maine and being well acquainted with the fish and wildlife and because I knew every trick of the poacher, this would be all the qualifications I would need to nail down the job.

Off to Augusta I go to offer my services to this august body of law enforcement. This is where my education on the workings of the Maine Fish and Game department begins. In order to qualify for the exalted position of warden your knowledge must come from books, not from first hand knowledge and experience.

I have now come to the end of my career in law-enforcement.

There is an old saying that states, "if you can't lick, 'em, join 'em." I couldn't join 'em so I licked 'em.

I do not know if there is a statue of limitations on the game laws so this section will become the telling of tall tales.

I was taught to get my meat where I found it and that the game pays no attention whatsoever to calendars or clocks. Also, that the laws of survival supersede all other laws.

I will say here that I have never shot a deer after dark; I never had to. There were always plenty of deer around in the daytime.

In these tales, "Bub" is referring to my brother-in-law Ron Greenleaf. He was my partner in the camp and my partner in crime.

Game Management

In the early days of the Kelly Brook camp the fish and game were plentiful. Me and Bub figured that if we used our good judgment, this would always be so.

The game management that we practiced worked very well for most of the years that we had the camp.

The two beaver bogs on the brook were full of trout. We could have caught them by the hundreds, but we only took what we could eat.

When we had the kids with us I kept a set of flies with the barbs filed off so they could catch and release fish without killing them.

The partridge were so thick that there were flocks of them like hens all over the woods. The limit set by the state at that time was: 7 birds, but we only took 2 apiece.

We shot only male deer unless someone was in need of meat in a bad way.

Until the explosion of predators, clear-cutting and the spraying of toxic chemicals, we had a better program of game management than the State of Maine.

Sunday Hunting

Of all the idiotic laws enacted by idiots, the law banning Sunday hunting in the state of Maine is right up there close to the top of the list. Hunting is just about the only thing you cannot do. Drinking, smoking, gambling, fishing, playing sports, shooting at targets, these things can all be done legally but whatever you do, do not shoot at game.

The hunting season in Maine is so short that the average working man or woman who is only able to hunt on Saturdays will be luck to get in three days of deer hunting. If the weather is bad on any of these three days the state of Maine tells you, "tough luck."

Of course, the state is not concerned so much with the native Maine hunter; their interest lies with those people, (not from around here.) The thinking here is that they bring a lot of cash into the state. I, for one, have never seen any of this easy money.

We at the brook basically ignored these stupid laws. A weeks hunt meant a full week. The last I knew, every week has a Sunday in it.

I myself chose not to hunt on Sunday as I enjoyed the day off. Sunday was a day for me to catch up on camp chores, do some cooking and knock back a few beverages.

The boys who had to return to work on Monday chose to Sunday hunt, after all Sunday was one of their days off.

It is said that what you don't know can't hurt you. The wardens did not know so we did not get hurt. No one knew but us.

Every state that I have visited allows Sunday hunting. Why does the State of Maine keep us in the dark ages?

Rise up all ye hunters, let's band together and make some changes.

The Blaze Orange Law

At the time this law was passed, I believed that it was just another of those stupid laws to aggravate us hunters that were endowed with a little common sense. I knew that whoever was behind the passing of this law had never hunted in their life and only wanted to save us from ourselves.

I knew that there was no way I could get close to a deer all lit up like a Christmas tree. At first I consented to wear a band of orange around my green hat, then the state said you need more so I had my wife sew orange tape down the seams of my pants. This was soon not enough to suit the powers that be. I finally ended up wearing a hat and coat of this loud color.

I will now admit I was wrong about this law, it has saved lives and I get just as close to deer as I have always done.

The state however could not stop there, they seem to think that they have to diddle around a law until it becomes totally unreasonable. They have gone too far as usual.

My best friend and hunting partner gave me a blaze orange parka. This is a very expensive coat. It has a fur collar, a game pocket and many other features and is the warmest coat I have ever owned by far.

The all-powerful state says I cannot wear this coat while hunting. Even though this coat shows up in the woods like a neon sign, because there is a camouflage pattern on it, it is illegal. This is just another example of taking a law too far. If the coat is highly visible to other hunters it should be legal.

I have had to buy an orange vest to go over the coat. The people that I hunt with say, that the vest makes no difference in the coats visibility.

If we could only fire the people that we hire to work for us in managing the fish and game department we would maybe be able to undo some of this foolishness.

As I mentioned before, we enacted our own bucks only law, however we put not restrictions on the length of the horns. To do this would have made no sense at all and would have done nothing to keep the deer herd in our area stable.

Read on to find out how the State of Maine in all their wisdom, wrote their law, a law by the way that is impossible to comply with.

The Tape Measure Law

The State of Maine with perfect hind-sight decided to lock the barn door after the horse had been stolen. This law was passed after the coyotes, wolves and the spraying of Agent Orange all over the woods, had reduced the deer herd to dangerous levels.

The Bucks only Law was at the time about the only way to fix this state of affairs. This was good but those mental midgets who make the laws couldn't stop there. They had to play with and add to this law, I think just to justify their reason for being. It was decided that for a male deer to be legally taken, the horns must be 3 inches long.

Even though I carried a tape measure with me at all times on my hunts, I never found even one deer that would stand still long enough for me to measure his horns. The deer seemed to resent all this fooling around. The game had changed, however. Instead of shooting, the hunters were now measuring and this was not playing by the rules of the hunt.

I know of one insane instance where an old lady looking to supplement her Social Security check with a little extra meat, was arrested and fined because her deer's horns measured only 2 ¾ inches. If this don't give you a "wake-up-call" as to what is happening in this state, your not paying attention.

Instead of listening to those of us who live out here with these animals and know what is going on in the woods, the state hires college graduates who once saw a picture of a deer in a textbook. I am helping to pay the wages of these so-called experts but I don't have the option of firing them for their screw-ups. In the private sector these people would not last a week.

There are so many game laws on the books today that if you want to stay legal while hunting or fishing, hire a lawyer or better yet, marry one, or sleeping with one might work. Take this lawyer with you when you venture fourth on your hunting or fishing trips.

Let's Weigh the Bear Law

This was the most stupid law ever pushed on to the hunters of Maine. This law required the hunter to make sure that a bear weighed over 50 lbs. before shooting it.

Anyone who has hunted knows that a bear in the woods looks much bigger than it really is. The people who think up these laws have never seen a bear in the woods.

Being the law-abiding hunter that I have always tried to be, I made a set of scales part of my hunting kit, also a bag, as this was the only way I could think of to get a bear on to the scales. (Stuff the bear into the bag and then set it onto the scales.) The trouble I had trying to perform this operation you can imagine (the bear clawed the Hell out of me.) Rather than having to buy a new wardrobe and a new bag every time that I encountered a bear I decided to give up bear hunting altogether.

Three cheers for the chairperson of the board on bear management. At least one of the people who passed this law must have been a bear hunter as this law was later repealed. They must have gotten tired of buying new clothes too.

Seceding from the Union

On one of our resupply trips to the brook, Bub and me being in our cups so to speak and being totally unhappy with all the rules and regulations that seemed to be stripping us our freedom, decided that we would make the Kelly Brook area a separate country. The camp would be its capitol.

Knowing how the good old U.S. of A. deal with its defeated enemies, we figured we could declare war on the United States and before a shot could be fired in anger we would run up the white flag and surrender.

Now we would become entitled to "war reparations." Millions of dollars would flow in to our national treasury and we could live at the camp year around, hunting, fishing, trapping and making up our own laws as we went along.

The only problem that we could see arising from all of this would be talking the girls into moving in to camp with us.

This would become a job for the U.N. to solve.

Another Dream that Never Bore Fruit...

Kelly Brook Bow and Bird Hunt

One fall just before the firearms season for deer was slated to begin, I figured a little extra time at camp was just what the doctor would order-if I could afford a doctor that is. I would be removing myself from bill collectors, TV, telephones and all the rest of the burdens people have to cope with to attain the American dream.

I packed my gear and with my bow and my rifle, I took myself off to Kelly Brook. Just think: three whole days, all alone. If we could bottle this time and sell it, we would become very rich indeed.

I spent the first afternoon working around camp; spaced frequently by beverage breaks and planning my next days hunt. My goal was to have meat on the game pole by the time the boys came in on Saturday.

I spent a very pleasant morning roaming the woods but had no meat to show for my efforts. At noon I returned to camp for some lunch and to rethink my meat plans. On reaching the camp I observed 8 partridge scratching in the front yard like a bunch of chickens in a barnyard. I had no arrows for small game with me but in the camp under the mattress was a 12ga. sawed off shotgun.

This shotgun was only 16 inches long overall and was I to be caught with this in my possession I would be writing this from a Federal pen.

The only way to reach the gun is to walk right thru these dumb birds who seem to think they are hens. There is nothing to do but do it. I'm thinking these birds are going to leave the country as soon as I make my move. "Not these birds." They fly up into a popular tree not 40 feet from the camp door and go to roost like the hens that they think they are.

With one shell in the gun, two in my mouth and three in my hand, I make my stalk from the bed to the camp door. Taking aim on the lowest bird in the tree I shoot and the two bottom birds fall (did I mention that this shotgun has one wicked pattern spread?) I load up another round and drop the next bird. All this time these birds are still acting like chickens.

Six of the eight birds became camp meat. The other two decided that maybe they should be somewhere else. They landed down the brook a little ways and if I had had me a real gun I might have taken them too.

I dressed out my birds and put them in the brook to cool. I just had to have one for my supper but the rest I hung on the game pole just before the boys came in. They couldn't claim that there was no camp meat waiting for them.

Living off the Land

One September weekend, fishing season being over and bird season still a couple of weeks away, Bub and me decided to pack some supplies in to camp and work up some wood for the coming deer season.

Friday afternoon we hiked in, stowed our gear and as it is the custom on arriving at camp, we enjoyed a few beverages. Because we had a lot to pack in we didn't bring along much grub. A dozen eggs, a pound of bacon and some butter. Kelly Brook offered plenty of grub for a couple of enterprising young lads.

Bub being a fella who thinks much of his stomach, wants to know, "what's for Saturday night supper?"

Now Saturday night up here in Maine is known as the "night of the three b's: being: "beer," "beans" and "bath" night. The bath is out of the question, however, the beer and the beans are doable.

While whipping up a batch of biscuits I put the beans on to soak. Because we had no salt pork I had to use half of the bacon for the beans.

Friday night's supper was biscuits and molasses and coffee. This was the last of our molasses. I now have a problem with the beans. We mulled this over for a while and Bub says, "we got maple syrup." This went into the beans. I know that these beans are coming out of the oven the same color as they went in: white. The left over breakfast coffee is the only thing I can think of for color. This coffee was about the same consistency as molasses and about the same color. Into the beans it goes and into the oven.

We work on the woodpile all morning and then retired to the camp for a beverage break.

Bub, thinking of his stomach as usual, says "we should have a partridge for the bean pot." Bub had strapped on his Ruger Bearcat pistol in case we were attacked by varmints. This little 22 could be fired in your pocket and never put a hole in your pants. I told Bub to go down the brook and get us a bird and I would take the fly-rod and go down to the beaver bog and catch us some trout for our Sunday breakfast. The bog just teemed with pan-sized trout so I kept a rod and flies in the camp.

I had myself 12 nice fish and was sitting by the brook cleaning them when I heard Bub shoot 6 times. I looked down the brook and there was Bub waving at me to come down and pointing at the alders. When I reached him, he says look in the bushes. There was a bird about 10 ft. from us and the bird acted like it was in a state of shock. Bub hands me the pistol and says, "you try; I can't hit it." Down on my belly I go and worm my way thru the alders until I am just 5 ft. from this scared to death bird.

Taking a careful aim at the bird's body, I shot it in the head. Of course I told Bub that this was the way I planned it.

I dressed the bird, picked up the fish and back to camp we go to celebrate these events with one or three beverages. I bone the bird and added it to the bean pot. Bub claimed that these were the best beans I had ever baked. This could have been due to the fact that everything tasted better at camp, or it could have maybe been due to the consumption of numerous beverages.

After this experience I took an old 12ga. shotgun into camp and left it just for these times of need.

The Rape of the Land

There were flocks of partridge all up and down the brook and the bogs were teeming with fish. Pan size trout just right for eating.

The state limit on birds at the time was 7. We limited ourselves to just 2 each. We could have taken fish by the basket full. We only took what we could eat.

We made our own bucks only law but if one of us needed meat we would allow a doe to be taken. In all the years we hunted the area we never took a doe.

These self-imposed rules worked very well and we always had an abundant supply of fish and game.

Due to the mismanagement practices of the fish and game department and the rape of the land by the paper companies, the area was turned into a vast wasteland.

The beaver have left the area as the loggers left them nothing to eat. I don't think there is a trout left from one end of the brook to the river.

About 10 years ago I went in to camp to do a little bird hunting. I never saw a bird, nor did I see any sign of any having been there. There was very little deer sign to be seen either.

Bub's kids use the camp now for ATVs and snowmobiling. The hunting and fishing is no more.

Labor Day Groceries

This story takes place sometime about the middle sixties, a great time to be alive.

Ron, better known as "Bub," had gone over to New York State to work on a line crew. While there he met and got hitched to a very nice young lady. For a wedding present, the company he worked for gave him the dreaded, "pink slip." Bub with his new bride packed up his dunnage and he and his new bride and came back home to Maine. His New York rocking-chair money did not arrive with him. This is better known as "unemployment insurance." Why it is called this I could never understand as it does not insure against unemployment. Bub is living proof of this.

They found an apartment and set up housekeeping. Two months later no check had arrived from New York and the pantry is getting bare. Bub asks can we take a trip to camp and get the honeymooners some meat.

It's coming up on Labor Day weekend so we decide to take the girls and make a three-day hunt. We made up four packs just so the girls would not feel left out of all the fun. Bub took his 32-40. I took a 30-cal. carbine that I had traded for and wanted to try out. This cal. is a little small for deer but with the scope I had put on it I figured I could place my shot.

I was also thinking that if we were caught and the state was going to take my rifle, this was the rifle I would want them to take.

On arriving at camp and tossing back a few of our favorite beverages, we planed the next day's hunt.

Since we did not want to take two deer, we decided that Bub would hunt in the morning and I would hunt the afternoon. We also decided, "no big deer" as getting it out under the eyes of a warden could become a problem.

We got up the next morning to a heavy rain and Bub took off on his hunt. About 10:00 am I went out back of the camp to do what nature was asking of me. Coming down the knoll towards me was a little deer. I decided that since I hadn't heard Bub shoot that I would take this deer as it was just the size we were looking or. Back to the camp I go for my carbine and when I get back the deer is laying down and I can't get a clean shot. Knowing that deer just like a dog will make more than one bed before they get it just right, I waited. Sure enough this little fella gets up and proceeds to go around in circles looking for the perfect bed. When the angle is right I put one in his neck just back of the head. He just stands there. I know these 30 cal. carbines were not made for stopping power but this deer should be down. I can see the hole where I had hit him thru the scope.

I fire once more and another hole appears right next to the first one. The deer is still standing there and is not moving even a little bit. Something is very wrong here. Once more I fire. There stands the deer with another hole in his neck. I have a very nice group of three but I guess no one has told the deer this. Walking slowly up to this deer I am ready to cross-stitch him with the 12 shots I have left in the clip. When I reach the deer I find that he has hung himself on a limb stub sticking out from a fir tree. There was no way he could fall even if he had wanted to. He was my deer after the first shot.

Bub came back when he heard me shoot, as he knew what the meat problem was taken care of. We dressed, skinned it out and deboned it and hunt the meat in the shade until we were ready to leave. Of course a few beverage breaks were taken during this job of work. We had maybe 40lbs. of clear meat to pack out.

After a pleasant three days at camp, it came time to return home. I have always hated these times.

From past experience we know if there is to be a warden in our future he will be waiting at the car when we get there. This would spoil our trip, big time. My criminal mind now comes into play.

Bub will take the girls and the packs out to the car. I will take the meat up over the ridge to an old logging road in the opposite direction and wait for Bub and the girls to drive around and if there is no one about I will step out into the road when I hear him toot the horn one short toot.

We made it back home without meeting any new friends in uniform. Crime has paid off again.

The next day Bub called to tell me that his checks had finally arrived. Me and the wife were invited to supper. Some deer steak, a good wine and good companions; who said life ain't great?

Figure 18: The girls on the Labor Day hunt: Bub's wife Bea holding the dog; my wife Corrine, probably holding her temper.

The Kelly brook area was over-run with moose. You could most always see five or six on every hunt.

These next moose stories were totally unplanned events. No one in their right mind would ask for all the work required to get a moose out of that remote area on their backs.

When ever an Indian shot a moose he would move his house to the moose instead of the moose to the house. This makes a lot of sense to me as the bulk of the work on these moose hunts fell largely to me.

The Great Kelly Brook Moose Hunt

This is going to be a very long story folks although it was longer in the doing than it will be in the telling.

Bub has this friend that he has known since they were just young lads in school. This pal of Bubs quit the hallowed halls of learning to work for the U.S. Army where he made his mark as an expert with any weapon that Uncle Sam would let him borrow.

After spending several years in the big green machine he came home to stay. The first thing he wished to do was go on a deer hunt. He claimed he would like to shoot at something that did not shoot back.

Bub called me to see about taking him to the camp for a few days. I had my gear packed, kissed my wife goodbye and was out the door before he could hang up the phone. (Any excuse to go to camp, deer hunting would do.

I guess Bub mention to his pal just what going to camp entailed because when we picked up he had enough gear packed to spend a month in deepest Africa.

After separating the wheat from the chaff so to speak, we got him squared away and off to camp we went.

We reached the camp Saturday afternoon. Now there is a hard and fast rule that when opening the camp, beverages must be consumed. This is about the same as launching a ship only we didn't break the bottles until after they were empty. There is also a hard and fast rule that there will be no hunting if beverages are consumed. There was no hunting done on this first day.

Bub's chum had purchased himself an army surplus rifle, not our army but something I think that that came from a Third World country. A box of ammo cost more than the rifle. I couldn't tell just which end of the thing done the killing. However he claimed it to be a mighty fine deer gun. There is another hard and fast rule that says you do not bad mouth a man's deer gun.

Figuring that he had a lot of hunting days owed to him, Sunday was just as good a day as any for deer hunting so off he goes. Bub and me stayed at camp, Bub doing camp chores and me doing a lot of cooking, both of these jobs requiring numerous beverage breaks.

Along about noon we heard a shot quite a way's off and in the wrong direction. It looks like there will be a job of work ahead of us.

Game shot down the brook was already between the camp and the trucks and this was easier to deal with when it came time to pack up and leave. Game shot up the brook had to be dragged back to camp, hung on the game pole and then dragged to the trucks. This shot was up the brook.

Me and Bub are thinking that our laid-back Sunday has just been ruined.

About two hours later in comes the source of our worries with a smile on his face that is hard to describe.

I can't see any blood on him and no heart and liver so maybe that gun of his shoots as bad as it looks.

Now it becomes: "we said," "he said." We said, "did you get him?" He said, "yes." We said, "how big?" He said, "really big." We said, "how far away?" He said, "about a mile or two, (it was two.)" We said, "how much does it weigh?" He said, "7 or 800lbs, (it was closer to 900lbs.)" We said, "OH, NO!"

This calls for a meeting of the board. I will not let meat go to waste but right about now I was wishing that gun of his shot as bad as it looked.

We are talking about one hell of a lot of meat. It would take four miles of backpacking and a forty-mile trip home without making the acquaintance of any officers of the law.

The deer hunting is now over for this trip and the work begins.

We spend the rest of the day sharpening knives and consuming copious amounts of beverages and cussing a lot.

The next morning, bright and early with pack-baskets, garbage bags and every knife we own, we headed up the brook in a rainstorm that was coming down in sheets.

"Who needs this?" I ask no one in particular, with more added that I won't repeat here. Cussing was definitely called for at this time.

We finally reach the scene of this foul deed and now I am thanking the mother of us all for this storm. This animal is as big as a horse; with horns you could paddle a canoe with, laying in a chopping where every airplane in North America will have a birds-eye view of this operation. I want very badly to get this moose under the trees and out of sight but the three of us can just about lift the head. The rest of him won't budge.

Anyone reading this please pay close attention to what happens next if you are planning to shoot a moose, legal or otherwise.

Bub's good old buddy had decided that shooting the thing was all that was required of him and the rest was up to me.

I slit the hide the length of the backbone and down the quarters like peeling a banana. Getting my fingers under the loins I striped them away from the spine and Bub put these in a garbage bag. This part of the operation dulled three knives so we put our shooter of moose to sharpening knives. After stripping the cuts of meat from the quarters we rolled the animal over and repeated the process.

We now have 12 garbage bags full of meat and three of us to pack them back to camp.

With all of us dragging the carcass, we manage to tug it into the woods and cover it with brush. This entire procedure took under an hour, (I don't dilly-dally when I am breaking the law.

With pack baskets full we start for camp. Sweating and cussing is the order of the day.

We had not gone very far before we realized we were over loaded. Breaking out some more bags we redistributed the loads.

The rain is coming down even harder than before and soaked to the skin with our tails dragging we finally reach camp. The boys got me into this mess and they would not be getting off that easy. "Boys," I says, "all of that meat has to be at the camp before we can quit, if not the varmints will get it and all this work will be for nothing." After what I have been thru, not an ounce of this meat will be lost.

It was long after dark before we had all the meat back at camp and hung in the loft to start the aging process.

Soaked to the skin we peeled off our clothes and discovered we were all wearing red long johns. The blood from the meat had soaked thru our clothes. It took two days to dry them out and it was all for nothing as it rained for six days.

On the third day we packed what meat we could lug and leaving everything else at camp we headed for the truck. The brook has become a river, so we just wade through as we are already as wet as we will ever get.

Forty miles to home and safety; I can picture in my mind a roadblock every five miles. My nerves are starting to get just a little frayed.

We arrive home safe and sound with out having to talk with any members of the warden service. After hanging the meat in the cellar we returned to camp, all of this in the pouring rain.

Figuring that if we was to eat some of the meat we wouldn't have to lug it, at least not on our backs, we cooked up about 8lbs. of steak and pigged out. This was after a few beverages to stimulate our appetites.

4 four more trips to the truck had removed all the evidence from the camp, after another feed of steak to lighten the loads a bit.

Now we need to make another trip for our rifles and the rest of our gear, all of this as the rain comes down. Our long johns are now dyed red forever.

Another trip home without becoming closely associated with the officers of the law.

The meat is now hanging in my cellar aging nicely. I am warm and dry and back in the arms of my loving family, although my wife is not too happy with me at this time.

We more or less fractured the game laws on this deer hunt but the meat fed three families for most of the winter. No one needed food stamps or welfare so maybe we saved the state some tax money.

I was taught in school that the people are the state. If this is so and if the fish and game belong to the state, then they rightfully belong to all of us.

Maybe this has changed since I was in school? I have never bothered to ask.

Baby Bear & Second-Hand Smoke

This was a year when we saw a bumper crop of beechnuts. You could scoop them up by the hand full, which I did.

I was working a beech ridge in search of the elusive whitetail deer. About 10 AM, I had the urge to sit myself down, eat some beechnuts and have myself a pipe. I had just gotten settled in and my pipe going good when off to my left I heard the damnedest goings on that I have ever heard in all my years in the Maine woods. I could see sticks and leaves flying up in the air from behind a brush pile and every now and again a halfhearted screech. I had no idea what was causing all of these goings on.

After a few minutes of this shattering of the peace and quiet in my little corner of the world, out comes a baby bear and tears up over the ridge like his tail was on fire. This made me very happy. Not only would I get my peace and quiet back, but I wanted nothing to do with mama bear. I had already shot a nice sized boar bear the week before and that would be all the bear steaks that I would be needing for one year.

No sooner had this little fella left when the leaves and sticks started to fly up in the air again. After a bit out comes baby bear; no, two. This little fella has no plans to follow baby bear number one. He takes a hard right turn and proceeds to crowd my space.

I watch him coming towards me all the time keeping a sharp eye out for mama. I am puffing on my pipe as he steps over my legs with out giving me the time of day. A few feet more and he puts on the brakes, turns around, sits down and stares at me all the while cocking his head from side to side. Back he comes up to my legs where he proceeds to start the head cocking business again.

Now, I don't know if any of you folks have ever been up close to a real live bear. If you have you know all about the smell. This baby's breath was nothing like any baby breath I had ever smelled and his brand of deodorant was not working at all.

I am now getting more than a little worried about where mama bear is right now. Now wanting her to show up and spoil a very fine day I started blowing pipe smoke into the face of this little fool.

Now this idiot bear cub took to that pipe smoke like a duck does to water. The more I puffed and blew the more he sniffed. As I am not wanting to become pals with no bear large or small I start talking to him. This don't seem to bother him any so I am thinking maybe touching him will send him on his way. No such luck. He seems to be here to stay and wanting me to start adoption proceedings. This I really don't need. Just having this guy breath on me was making me forget all about eating any beechnuts. Since he don't seem to want to leave I decide that I will be the one to go. This is not to be. Here he comes, waddling along behind, talking bear talk at every step. I either have to get rid of him, or forget deer hunting for the day and take him back to camp for a mascot.

Now a hunting camp smells bad enough without adding this new odor to the mix, what with beer farts, unwashed long johns and other goings on. Turning around I wave my hat in his face and yell as loud as I can. Now he thinks I want to play and starts rolling around and doing his leaf tossing act all over again. Maybe he thinks I am his mama, after all I ain't smelling so good either after a week at camp.

This foolishness goes on for the rest of the morning and the light bulb goes off in my head: I will take him back to where bear number one was last seen and maybe the scent of his buddy with all the brains in the family weren't the scent of his pal will smell better to him than I do. This stroke of genius is the answer. As soon as he got the scent he took off up the ridge like he had a fire lit under his butt. I never saw him again nor smelled him, neither.

This was just another of those special times that can be found in the woods of Maine.

If there is any moral to this story it is maybe: be careful who you make friends with while in the woods, "mama could be watching."

As old Roy used to say, "happy trails."

As you by now can tell, I am very partial to all of them "old-timers."

Most of what is found in this book would not be possible with out their teachings.

There were three kinds of old-timer: those that obeyed the game laws, those that bent the game laws just a wee bit and those that downright fractured them. This next tale is about one of the latter. The names and places have been changed to protect the innocent.

I will call him "Dead River Fred."

The Old-Timer & The Long Arm of the Law

This old timer was the number one poacher in the area and he had never been caught, though not for the want of trying. To the Maine wardens he was Public Enemy #1.

Old Fred figured that what was in the woods and waters that he loved was put there for his use and a full belly was the only law that he obeyed. He knew that those idiots down to Augusta had nothing better to do than sit around and figure out ways to keep him from eating his three squares once a day.

On a nice summer's day, it just happening to be a Saturday, this old boy decides to take himself to town for some beer and conversation, two things that was lacking in his life most of the year.

The afternoon turned to evening, the evening turned to night. The beer turned to something quite a bit stronger, what is called up in this neck of the woods, "Old Stump Blower." This stuff could strip the varnish off a cedar canoe.

Our hero now decided to get himself back to camp as he has many miles of dirt road to travel before he sleeps.

Enter now Maine's newest addition to the warden service. This young fella is all decked out in his brand new uniform, spit and polish from head to toe, all puffed up and full of himself. He is thinking that if he can put the arm on old Fred it would be a good career move. Our intrepid hero of the law parks himself on a logging road not to far from Fred's cabin waiting to catch him with his ill-gotten gains, namely illegal meat or fish.

Now our brand spanking new officer of the law is getting very hot and sweaty as he can't roll down the truck windows because he will be eaten alive by those flying tigers of the Maine woods known as black flies. Being a civilized type person he has on all of the sweet smelling stuff such as shaving lotion, deodorant, etc. Black flies just love people that smell pretty.

Along about midnight he sees old Fred weaving his way down the road on his way home. Making his first dumb move he places his truck across the road directly in Fred's path. Remember Fred is carrying quite a load.

Luck is riding with the law this night. Fred comes to a stop inches from that nice shiny belt buckle. Our boy come very close to adding a warden to his list of trophies.

This brand new warden figures he has got old Fred dead to rights and will have the cuffs on him in short order; visions of promotion and financial gain dance in his head. Removing Fred from his truck he proceeds to poke and pry in Fred's truck all the time swatting black flies and sweating buckets. For his efforts he finds nothing. The fly bites have his face looking like last month's Hamburg.

Now just because Fred is called "Dead River" does not mean that he has anything to do with water, in fact he is allergic to it in all its forms. It has been many moons since Fred has given any thought to a bath and then that is as close as he has come to doing it. Fred's clothes have never seen a washing, as he believed this would cause them to wear out quicker. All of this made Fred Quite ripe. The town's people gave old Fred plenty of room and so did those damned black flies.

Fred was having a great old time watching this young fool suffer.

The warden now asks, "why don't these flies bother you none?" "Well, Sonny," says Fred, "them's just circle flies and don't bother a body much." "Circle flies? I never heard of them kind of flies before," says Sonny boy. "Them's flies that circle around a horses ass," says Fred.

"Are you calling me a horses ass?" says the warden.

"No, Sonny," says Fred. "I would never call you a horses ass, but them flies seem to think you are."

On this note, with no culprit in cuffs and a small amount of wisdom our warden takes himself back to civilization and takes up chasing married woman. The flies are not so thick and the smell is much nicer.

Old Dead River Fred has passed over to that poacher's paradise in the sky but he still lives with me everyday and his teachings will stay with me until I join him on our next hunt.

Figure 19: This moose decided to spend a little time on our target range. He was very lucky that he became a picture instead of my winters' meat.

The End

I guess I have come to the end of this epic saga of the north woods. I hope there is never really an end. These were the best years of my life.

Everyone that had the Kelly Brook experience still talks of those times. The memories I hope will last from generation to generation.

Both of my kids have done very well in life and the times we spent together is at least part of the reason for this.

If you enjoy the woods and waters of Maine and don't have a deer camp, I strongly recommend one as a place to become close to your family--the more rustic the camp the better.[19]

---

[19] One last tip: There are usually a lot of snakes around a deer camp so make sure you have a snakebite kit on hand. This should be about 100 proof.

Acknowledgements

Special thanks to:

-Lynn Greenleaf for giving us the camp.

-Ron & Bea Greenleaf, Ron, Jr. & family

-Sandy Savage for all the work on the computer

-Gerry Savage, Gerry, Jr., Red Daigle, Dave McLaughlin and my son, Dave, for all the good times

A lot of hands have helped in the production of this book. Jason Blood typed the electronic manuscript. The proofing was done by Sumner Hayward. All the organization and editing for the final manuscript were done by Paul and Sue at Kennebec Fox.

Index

List of Figures

7222360R0

Made in the USA
Lexington, KY
05 November 2010